PREFACE

WE first published a book with this title in 1947. Since then there have been vast changes in the U.S. and world economies, especially in the financial markets.

Six decades ago, a phrase such as "sound as a dollar" would not have had the ironic ring it would today. At that time, Americans were conditioned to believe that the dollar was "as good as gold." Most people's nest eggs were made up of savings accounts, savings bonds, life insurance policies (or even in currency hoarded in mattresses and cookie jars). Such fixed-dollar claims paid relatively low interest rates. Interest on passbook savings accounts, for example, was typically calculated on the minimum balance during a quarter (which meant that any funds withdrawn, or deposited during a calendar quarter did not earn any interest), and posted at the end of the quarter. This simplified the computation of interest, but made the effective rate on an account in which there was any activity less than the stated interest rate.

Today, there is a wide variety of fixed-dollar instruments available to the average citizen, including money market funds and accounts, upon which checks may be written, with interest accrued on the daily balance. These, and much more that we now take for granted, were made possible by advances in information technology. The increased speed and accuracy of data processing has facilitated complex financial transactions, even in small amounts, and greatly lowered their costs. This trend, as well as increasing affluence, has broadened the ownership and even the forms of financial assets held by the general public.

In 1947, direct and indirect ownership of common stocks was limited to a relatively small minority of the public. Brokerage commissions were fixed at high levels. Funded pension plans were in their infancy and there were only a few hundred or so mutual funds in operation. Open-ended funds generally carried sales loads. In the United States today, there are more than 8,000 mutual funds devoted to common stocks alone (more, in fact, than the number of publicly-traded U.S. companies). Well over half of households now own stocks directly or indirectly via mutual funds, pension plans and variable annuities.

These changes have been in part a response to the most fundamental change of all since 1947—the relentless erosion of the purchasing power of the dollar. Since we first published "How to Invest Wisely," the dollar has lost nearly 90 percent of its value and there is no end in sight.

This has meant that everyone concerned with maintaining the purchasing power of savings is forced to accept risks, often risks that they do not understand, and that their forebears would not have undertaken. What most people call investing today is, in fact, speculation, based on the hope that oneself or someone one has hired can identify assets that are somehow mispriced in the market place. All too often this leads to chasing after one financial fad after another—"driving in the rear-view mirror"—with disappointing results.

The first four chapters of this book are devoted to very basic and timeless principles of preserving and enlarging wealth, such as living within one's means, minimizing transaction costs (principally by purchasing assets rather than having them sold to you), and understanding risks. The rest of the book is based on relatively recent academic findings concerning financial markets. Specifically:

1. That, over the long term, returns on financial assets are related to the risks involved
2. That the market prices of financial assets reflect potential returns and risks
3. That it is folly to believe that anyone can consistently evaluate those returns and risks more accurately than the market
4. That financial assets can be classified into groups whose constituents behave more like one another than like the constituents of other asset classes, and
5. That broad diversification among asset classes can reduce risk.

This book is designed to help you become an *investor* (rather than a speculator) with a sound and coherent plan and the discipline to stick to it. You will then be in a position to be fully compensated for the risks you decide to undertake.

Lawrence S. Pratt
Senior Fellow

Contents

PREFACE i

INTRODUCTION 1
Saving and Investing 1
Savings Programs 3
The Time to Invest 4

I. THINGS TO DECIDE AND DO 5
How Much Can You Invest? 5
Your Dollar Holdings 5
Tax-Exempt Securities 6
Holding Your Investments 7
Tax-Deferred Investing 8

II. THE INVESTOR'S DILEMMA 11
Inflating Forces Investors to Become Speculators 11
Principal and Income 14
Some Things Don't Change 15
Accepting Risk 16

III. UNDERSTAND AND AVOID NEEDLESS COSTS 19
Tangible Items 19
Real Estate 20
Securities 21
Mutual Funds 22
Pay Attention to Costs 23
Brokers, Investment Advisers and Financial Planners 25

IV. UNDERSTANDING RISK 27
Does Standard Deviation Equal Risk? 30
Fixed-Dollar Claims 32

V. ACTIVE VS. PASSIVE INVESTING 37
Index Funds 39
Risk and Return 40
Up From Stock Picking 42
Tax Efficiency 43

VI. THE WIDER MARKET 45
Other Indexes 46
Diversify to Control Risk 47

VII. THE BUILDING BLOCKS 51
Why Not the Best? 52
Gold and Gold Mining Companies 54
The Useless Middle 55
The Active Part of Passive Investing 56
What's Right for You? 57

VIII. BUILDING A PORTFOLIO 59
Why Rebalancing is Important 62

IX. WHY MOST INVESTORS FAIL 65
Skating to Where the Puck Was 65
Reasonable Expectations 66
Acting Like an Expert 68

APPENDIX A: THE HIGH YIELD DOW STOCK SELECTION STRATEGY 69
A Passive Approach 72
Why Just the Dow Jones Industrials? 73
Stable Dividend Policies are the Key 74
What About Growth Stocks? 76
What If Everyone Did It? 76
Discipline is Essential 77

APPENDIX B: SELECTED MUTUAL FUNDS 79

INTRODUCTION

THIS book is about investing: the patient and prudent management of financial assets for the long term. This book is not about starting or managing your own business or how to "get rich quick."

We have assumed that the management of investment capital is not the reader's primary occupation, either as the proprietor of a business or as a trader, dealer, or speculator. Our purpose is to help the reader develop a sound and systematic investment program that avoids major pitfalls, especially those arising from the emotionalism and fads of the marketplace.

Saving and Investing

Investing cannot be discussed sensibly without first discussing saving. This is because spending less for consumption than is possible with the resources at one's disposal is the *only* source of investable funds. Similarly, it is the *only* assured way of preserving, maintaining, and enhancing one's fortune.

This is the situation even if the bulk of your assets were received as a windfall in the form of an inheritance or winning the lottery. That you now have anything at all to invest reflects that you or your forebears did not spend all that was available.

For most people, saving is difficult because resources are limited while potential claims on them are not. Young families in particular often find themselves with significant debts in the form of education loans, home mortgages, and consumer credit for durable goods.

Those who find themselves in such a position should not be discouraged. Although it may not feel like it, repayment of debt is equivalent to saving, because reducing the amounts you owe increases your net worth just as adding funds to a savings account increases your net worth. Economists often call scheduled mortgage and automobile loan repayments "forced savings."

Debts that do not have a fixed payment schedule, so-called revolving credit accounts such as credit cards, typically bear the highest interest rates. Outstanding balances of this kind should be paid off before *any* funds are set aside as savings. Paying down credit-card balances is equivalent to putting funds in a savings account that pays the same rate of interest that the credit card company charges. If your credit-card company charges 1.5 percent per month (not deductible for income tax purposes) on your outstanding balance, then paying down that balance is equivalent to putting money in a tax-exempt savings account at more than 18 percent! It makes no sense to put money aside for emergencies when the returns offered in, say, a savings account are relatively low while paying interest charges at a higher rate on revolving credit account balances. In such circumstances, unused credit lines can be drawn down in emergencies.

Amortized loans such as most home mortgages and car loans requiring a fixed monthly payment that includes both an interest and principal repayment component can usually be repaid ahead of schedule. Adding an amount to the monthly payment to reduce the principal due will shorten the time left to repay the loan and greatly reduce the total interest paid over the life of the loan.

There are many government policies designed to encourage homeownership and to protect the investment of homeowners. These include the deductibility of mortgage interest from taxable personal income, as well as programs, tax breaks, and subsidies designed to encourage home mortgage lending at favorable rates. Most people should take advantage of these opportunities by accumulating funds for a down payment and purchasing their own home with a mortgage. Be sure that you understand the terms of the mortgage indenture and that the monthly payment, plus taxes, utilities, and maintenance cost, are within your means.

To repeat, principal repayments in excess of the required monthly mortgage payment have the same effect on one's long-term finances as putting the money in a savings account at the same rate of interest that you are being charged on the loan. However, because of the delays and expenses associated with refinancing such loans, accelerating principal repayments (paying extra each month) should only be undertaken after one has accumulated some cash reserves or arranged short-term credit lines for emergencies.

In general, whether it is better to repay debts or to accumulate savings will depend on the interest rate and whether the interest payments or the payments into savings are deductible from taxable income. If the *after-tax* outlays for interest are greater than the *after-tax* returns you expect to earn on your savings, then you should consider prepaying such loans.

Tax-deferred savings in an IRA, 401k, or a similar account may be advisable (see the box on p. 9) even when one is making payments on debts other than a home mortgage. Your contributions may be matched by your employer. Such plans use pretax dollars to accumulate funds, and investment income from such funds is not taxed as it is earned. There are usually some restrictions and possible penalties for withdrawals before reaching retirement age. Nevertheless, it may be possible to borrow from the account for purposes such as education, home purchase, or medical expenses. However, after-tax dollars must be used to repay such loans, with interest.

Savings Programs

The fundamental point remains: savings are the key to successful investing. When your debts are paid up, the soundest policy is to continue to add an amount equivalent to what you were paying on your debts to savings each month, rather than to increase your current consumption.

There are many other forms of forced savings besides scheduled debt repayments. These include whole-life insurance policies, employer pension and savings plans, payroll deductions to purchase U.S. savings bonds, and so on and so forth. This is not the place to discuss the pros and cons of such plans in detail.* However, tax-deferred pension plans warrant further comment here.

There are two types of employer-sponsored pension plans: defined-benefit plans and defined-contribution plans.

Defined-benefit plans typically provide for a retirement pension calculated as a percentage of your final salary for each year of service. It is up to the employer to make the contributions needed to fund such plans and the employer usually determines how the funds are invested. Employees typically have no discretion in defined-benefit plans, but, at a minimum, they should ascertain how much they can expect to receive at retirement and the extent to which their future benefits are vested (*i.e.*, whether they will receive anything if they cease to be employed by the company before they retire).

Under defined-contribution plans, specific funds are invested to provide for your retirement. Although these may be commingled with funds invested for others, there will be a specific portion that is for your retirement and your retirement alone. Your eventual benefits will depend on how much has been accumulated in your name and what has been earned on those investments. You will be required to direct how the funds are invested, but the choice is usually limited to broad categories of investments (these typically include short-term, money-market instruments, long-term bond funds, and common-stock funds of various types).

In contrast, funds held in self-directed pension plans, such as Individual Retirement Accounts (IRAs) and Keogh plans for self-employed persons, may be invested in nearly any way the beneficiaries direct.

---

* See AIER's books listed on the inside back cover for more information on this and other topics, especially *How to Build Wealth with Tax-Sheltered Investments* and *Life Insurance from the Buyer's Point of View*.

The Time to Invest

When beginning a savings program, conservative fixed-dollar holdings, such as insured passbook savings or certificates of deposit, should be used. During the first few years, the annual contributions (rather than investment performance) will account for most of the growth of the funds and needless risks should be avoided. In addition, the expenses associated with more complex or diversified investments cannot be justified when holdings are relatively small.

The same applies to funds accumulated toward large outlays that you can anticipate during, say, the next five years or so (such as buying a home or paying tuition). More generally, funds needed for day-to-day expenses and for emergencies should always be held in readily available form.

In any event, whether as a result of disciplined accumulation or as the result of a lump sum receipt (from a former employer or spouse, an estate, or a life-insurance policy, for example) the time may come when you find yourself with liquid assets in excess of what you need for anticipated outlays and emergencies. We presume that most readers of this book are in this position—they are now, or soon will become, investors.

I.
THINGS TO DECIDE AND DO

AS we shall see, a coherent strategy is essential to successful investing. Before developing such a strategy there are several things you will need to determine and consider, starting with a determination of what portion of your holdings you will devote to your investment portfolio and what portion is to be held in reserve for emergencies or for planned outlays in the near future.

How Much Can You Invest?

The place to begin is to list and appraise your current and probable future resources, and your current and future obligations. The reason for this exercise is not only to determine how much you have (it is amazing how inaccurate such estimates can be in the absence of a comprehensive and detailed appraisal), but also to determine how much you can prudently invest.

As we indicated in the introduction, funds for day-to-day expenses, reserves for emergencies, and accumulations for anticipated major outlays should be held in relatively liquid short-term, fixed-dollar claims (such as passbook savings or money-market funds). Reserves for emergencies should typically amount to six to 12 months' living expenses. Individual circumstances vary greatly and such holdings might be larger or smaller than this rule of thumb would indicate. For example, a married man with several dependents and whose major source of income is sales commissions should keep much larger reserves in relation to living expenses than, say, a widower on a military pension who lives next door to a Veterans Administration Hospital.

Similarly, accumulations toward items such as the down payment on a house or for college tuition for one's children that are likely to be needed within five years are best placed in fixed-dollar claims that will come due before the time of the anticipated outlay. It will be mainly the periodic contributions to such accumulations that will make them grow, and the risks involved in reaching for higher returns on more volatile types of assets are unwarranted.

Your Dollar Holdings

Although short-term, fixed-dollar claims are often inappropriate *investments* in a era of fiat currency, if you live and work in the United States, such claims are the appropriate vehicles for your working balances, reserves, and accumulations for foreseeable outlays. It may also happen that you will have to hold significant fixed-dollar claims when you are shifting among categories of investments, or when receipts accumulate pending investment or reinvestment, or for tactical considerations. When all of these are taken into account, your fixed-dollar holdings may well account for a significant portion of your total holdings.

Insured bank deposits are usually the most convenient for working balances. No more than the maximum insured amount of $100,000 per "category of legal ownership" should be deposited in any one bank. Deposits maintained in different categories (*e.g.*, single vs. joint accounts) are separately insured. Separate insurance is also available for IRAs and other retirement accounts. So, you can have more than $100,000 of insured deposits at a single bank. Note that the maximum applies to all deposits in a given category at a given bank, not to each bank account or certificate of deposit (CD). Ask your bank for this information.

We note that funds placed in bank CDs should have a range of maturities and interest rates. You will be less subject to interest rate fluctuations and, more significantly, if you need cash prior to maturity, you will only have to pay the penalty for early withdrawal on the portion you withdraw.

Money-market funds often offer the convenience of checking privileges. They are not insured and, accordingly, those money-market funds that invest in commercial paper, jumbo CDs, and other private instruments carry some degree of risk. "All Government" money-market funds that hold only U.S. Treasury obligations pay somewhat lower interest rates, but have very little risk.

Tax-Exempt Securities

The interest on municipal bonds (obligations of state governments and their political subdivisions) is not subject to direct Federal income taxes. However, receipt of such interest income can boost the taxes due from some taxpayers on their other income, and states that levy income taxes do not exempt interest receipts from other states.

Before considering municipal bonds, you should determine (preferably with the assistance of your accountant) not only what marginal income-tax rate (Federal, state, and local) you can expect to pay on taxable interest income, but if the effective rate on your other income would be increased if you received tax-exempt interest.

For most people, the interest from municipal bonds is equal to or less than what they would have in hand after paying taxes on taxable instruments of comparable maturity and risk. Thus, most investors will find that the major advantage of holding municipal bonds is the psychological satisfaction of paying less in taxes.

High-income taxpayers living in high-tax jurisdictions are the ones most likely to find municipal bonds or municipal-bond funds attractive. If fixed-dollar holdings are to be limited to the amounts needed for reserves, any advantages of municipal-bond holdings are likely to be offset by their lack of liquidity, as the spread between bid and asked prices of municipal bonds in the secondary market tends to be large. This lack of liquidity can be overcome to some extent via municipal-bond funds, but the expenses of such funds reduce their yield to the investor.

Holding Your Investments

You will also need to consider, or at least understand, the implications of how and where your investments are held.

You may hold assets as an individual or jointly with others (such as one's spouse or children). Assets may be held directly (tax-favored retirement accounts being a major exception) but receiving, holding, and delivering stock certificates and bonds and depositing dividend and interest checks, involves much tedious clerical work, which may be avoided by holding securities in a brokerage (or custodian) account. Assets may also be held in revocable or irrevocable trusts, etc. These decisions are often made in a haphazard fashion, but carry important implications for taxes, the ease (or difficulty) of administering your estate, as well as providing for children, especially in instances of divorce and remarriage. The issues involved are well beyond the scope of this book, but they should be thoroughly discussed with your lawyer and accountant, if only to give you an understanding of the possible ramifications of how your assets are titled and held.

You should take physical possession of tangible items, such as gold coins, that you acquire as investments. One of the major attractions of tangible items as investments is that they represent stores of value that are not dependent on anyone's promise and they cannot be seized with the stroke of a pen. Turning tangible stores of value over to a fiduciary or custodian thus defeats much of the purpose of acquiring them in the first place. Of course, theft will always remain a potential problem and such valuables should be held in a secure place.

Safe-deposit boxes, especially at institutions where you do not maintain other accounts and whose rental fees you do not claim as a deduction on your tax return, are preferable to home storage where the procedures for the disposition of valuables kept in your home after you die may well become "finders keepers," rather than those set forth in your will.

On the other hand, securities of any kind are simply pieces of paper. As such they depend on someone's explicit or implicit promise to pay you something in the future. Many investors prefer to take delivery of the securities they purchase and hold the certificates themselves. During the 1970s this was often recommended because of severe problems in the back offices of brokerage firms. However, such problems appear to have been largely overcome and, since the establishment of insurance protection, there have been no losses to customers from lost securities or broker insolvencies.

Moreover, and in contrast to 30 years or so ago, nearly all brokers now sweep dividends, interest, and sales proceeds into an interest-earning account, such as a money-market fund of the customer's selection, as soon as received. Keeping your negotiable securities in a brokerage account can thus relieve you of the clerical work of depositing checks and maintaining income-tax records—the broker will send to you a year-end statement for all interest and dividends received. If needed, the broker can be instructed to send to you accumulated funds or to deposit them directly into your checking account. Of course, the assets in tax-deferred accounts (such as IRAs) must be held by a broker or other custodian, so that you can prove to the tax collector that you have not spent the money.

As for the selection of a custodian, experience suggests that the quality of service seems to depend more on the local office you deal with than on the specific firm. For smaller retail accounts, there seems to be no discernible difference between discount and full-service brokerage firms in the accuracy and timeliness of statements, responsiveness to instructions, etc. On the other hand, bank custodians usually are less efficient and much more expensive than any broker. You not only have to pay the bank's fees, but also full commissions on any trades.

Needless to say, commissions and fees are higher at full-service brokers, but a more significant difference is that a discount broker will only execute your orders and will neither recommend trades nor attempt to sell to you issues they underwrite. This is often an advantage—brokers who depend on commission income for their livelihood may not always be willing to put your interests first. Unless you have established, and wish to maintain, a close relationship with an experienced and conscientious account executive, a discount-brokerage firm is usually the better choice.

Tax-Deferred Investing

If you are in a position to place funds in tax-deferred accounts, you should take full advantage of the opportunity to do so with your investment funds. (To repeat, these should only include resources for which you have no immediate plans.) The ability to accumulate investment income in this fashion serves to mitigate half of the double whammy (taxes—the other

It Pays to Start Early

The total return on investment is of primary significance in the absence of taxes. For example, the trustees of nonprofit institutions should focus on the amounts that can prudently be spent from the holdings in their endowment funds and not on whether the funds come from dividends, interest, rents, royalties, or capital gains.

The same applies to qualified (for tax-deferral of income taxes on funds set aside for retirement and the income thereon) pension plans of all kinds, in which any distributions are fully taxed no matter what their source. In particular, defined-contribution pension accounts held by individuals (IRAs, 401(k) plans, etc.), where the individual investor maintains control over the funds, provide investors with the opportunity to take advantage of the power of compounding over long periods.

It is unfortunate that most individuals do not set aside funds for retirement until they reach their late 40s or 50s. Starting much sooner can be very rewarding. For example, the total return on an IRA needs to be only about 2½ percent for an individual who contributes $20,000 at a rate of $2,000 per year beginning at 21, *and who never makes another contribution after the age of 30*, to have more at age 65 than someone who contributed $40,000 over 20 years starting at age 45. If the annualized total return on the two funds approximated the 12-percent gain achieved by common stocks over the past 50 years, the early bird would have about $1.8 million *vs.* about $144,000 for the late starter. If the early bird did not stop contributing at age 30, but continued to add $2,000 annually from age 31 to 65, it would only add another $900,000 to the funds available at age 65—about two-thirds of the $2.7 million total would reflect just the first 10 years of contributions compounded at 12 percent.

It usually is very difficult for 21-year olds to set aside funds in this manner. It even is difficult for 45-year olds. Nevertheless, the foregoing example indicates the extraordinary advantage of starting early. It also suggests that those who make annual gifts to children or grandchildren for estate planning purposes or other reasons might well suggest or even insist that the donees place as much as possible in tax-deferred pension accounts.

Finally, it should be noted that only relatively secure income-producing investments should be placed in tax-deferred pension accounts. One should resist the temptation to use such accounts for flyers on high risk investments in hopes of realizing large capital gains. It is the ability to increase the income earned within such accounts that gives them their potential, but if the value of your holdings decreases to zero, no amount of compounding can make them grow.

half is price inflation) faced by investors. Where possible, retired investors should make only the minimum mandatory withdrawals from tax-deferred accounts each year (i.e., the minimum required to avoid penalties). This will be zero for those under the age of 70 1/2. If additional funds are needed for living expenses, assets that are not in a tax-deferred account may be liquidated. This will allow funds to continue to accumulate on a tax-deferred basis—so that the taxes will become payable no sooner than necessary. However, those with large estates and substantial funds in tax-deferred accounts should seek competent advice in this regard, inasmuch as the amounts in tax-deferred accounts may be included in one's taxable estate and thus subject to income taxes when paid out to heirs.

Beware. The fact that capital gains are not taxed in tax-deferred accounts can create the temptation to take a flyer with such funds, say, by investing in high-risk growth stocks paying little or no dividends. While the prospect of not paying gains taxes on a stock that increases markedly in price might seem to make this appear sound, all too often such stocks decline toward worthlessness. In that event, the investor is often dismayed to find he cannot deduct the loss (conveniently forgetting that he received a deduction for the full amount invested when funds were paid into the account) and holds on to losers in the account in hopes of recovery.

The problem is that not even the miracle of compounding interest can make nothing increase to something. For this reason, investments in self-directed tax-deferred pension accounts should be concentrated in conservative holdings that offer generous current yields, which can compound and accumulate tax-free.

II.
THE INVESTOR'S DILEMMA

NEVER sell Consols," was the admonition of Mr. Forsyte in John Galsworthy's novel *The Forsyte Saga*. Consols, short for Consolidated Stock, are bonds of the British government. They were initially issued in 1751 to consolidate various debt issues of the British government. Consols were especially important in financing the Napoleonic Wars. They are perpetual annuities with no maturity date. They were long considered the safest and soundest of all investments and, along with similar high-grade, long-term bonds, were a foundation of the prosperity and comfort of propertied families such as the fictional Forsytes (derisively called "coupon clippers" because removing the interest coupons from their bonds was presumed to be their closest approximation of work).

Mr. Forsyte's dictum worked through the end of World War II. Since then, it has been a prescription for penury. The reason, of course, has been the rejection of sound currency by the governments of the world in favor of officially sponsored inflating.

Inflating Forces Investors to Become Speculators

Investing was a relatively simple matter when the British pound, the U.S. dollar, and other currencies were defined as and redeemable on demand in specific amounts of gold. Such currencies were generally believed to be as good as gold. High-grade bonds and similar instruments thus were even better than gold—they paid interest. The cost of living might go up or down with cycles of trade or of war and peace, but the long-term stability of prices seemed assured. Under a fully functional gold standard, long-term interest rates were quite stable through business cycles—interest rate fluctuations were far more pronounced in short-term than in long-term rates—and high-grade bond *prices* fluctuated in a relatively narrow range. In this environment, all an investor needed to do was save up some money and lend it out at interest to borrowers who were likely to pay it back.

This changed completely during the past century. The record of the British Consols (yes, you can still buy them) illuminates how much. The four percent Consols traded above par as recently as 1945, when the wholesale price level in Great Britain was (believe it or not) nearly the same as it was when Wellington defeated Napoleon at Waterloo. Since then, the British pound (and that perpetual stream of interest income from Consols) has lost more than 96 percent of its purchasing power.

This is an extreme example. Relatively few perpetual annuities such as British Consols have ever been issued—most high-grade bonds eventually mature and return 100 percent of par in terms of nominal currency, but the loss in purchasing power for these long-term investments over the past 60 years has rivaled Consols.

Chart 1 shows the long-term trend of the purchasing power of the dollar, which has decreased more than 90 percent since 1933. AIER has estimated that, through 2003, inflating cost savers in the United States more than half of the real wealth they had set aside and held in fixed-dollar claims. In 2003 dollars, these losses totaled more than $16 *trillion*.*

Fixed-dollar claims, other than currency itself, earn interest income for their holders, and interest rates on high-grade dollar instruments have at times included an inflation premium over the three or four percent that was usual in the days of the unquestioned gold standard. However, that premium has often been less than adequate to compensate investors in fixed-dollar claims for their losses in terms of purchasing power.

This is evident in Chart 2, which shows the cumulative value of $1.00 invested in 91-day U.S. Treasury bills from the end of 1953 through the end of 2006. Treasury bills are considered to be riskless in the sense that there is little doubt that the Treasury will repay them (with dollars created out of thin air if need be) and because they are very short term there is little risk their market value will decrease. It is very unusual for the market value of Treasury bills to be less that what their holders paid for them (and if it happens it is only by a very small amount and for a very short time). The rates on Treasury bills are usually comparable to what is available on savings accounts or money-market funds and similar risk-free holdings.

Also shown in Chart 2 are the cumulative values of that $1.00 adjusted for the cost of living as measured by the Consumer Price Index; the cumulative values after deducting income taxes each year (at an assumed tax rate of 35 percent); and the cumulative values after taxes and adjustment for the cost of living. The 50-year-average rates of return on each cumulative value series are also shown in the chart. The $1.00 grew to more than $14.00 over the 50-year period, an average return of 5.14 percent. But inflation averaging 3.88 percent per year reduced that amount to less than $1.90 (in terms of 1950 purchasing power) and the annual return to 1.21 percent.

If the interest earned each year had been taxed as it was earned (at an assumed rate of 35 percent) then the holder would have had a little less than $9.60 in the year 2006 the purchasing power of which would have been only about $0.67 in terms of 1950 purchasing power. The double whammy of

---

* See our bulletin "Stand Still, Little Lambs, to be Shorn," for the details of this grisly calculation.

Chart 1

Purchasing Power of the Dollar

(1792 = 1.00)

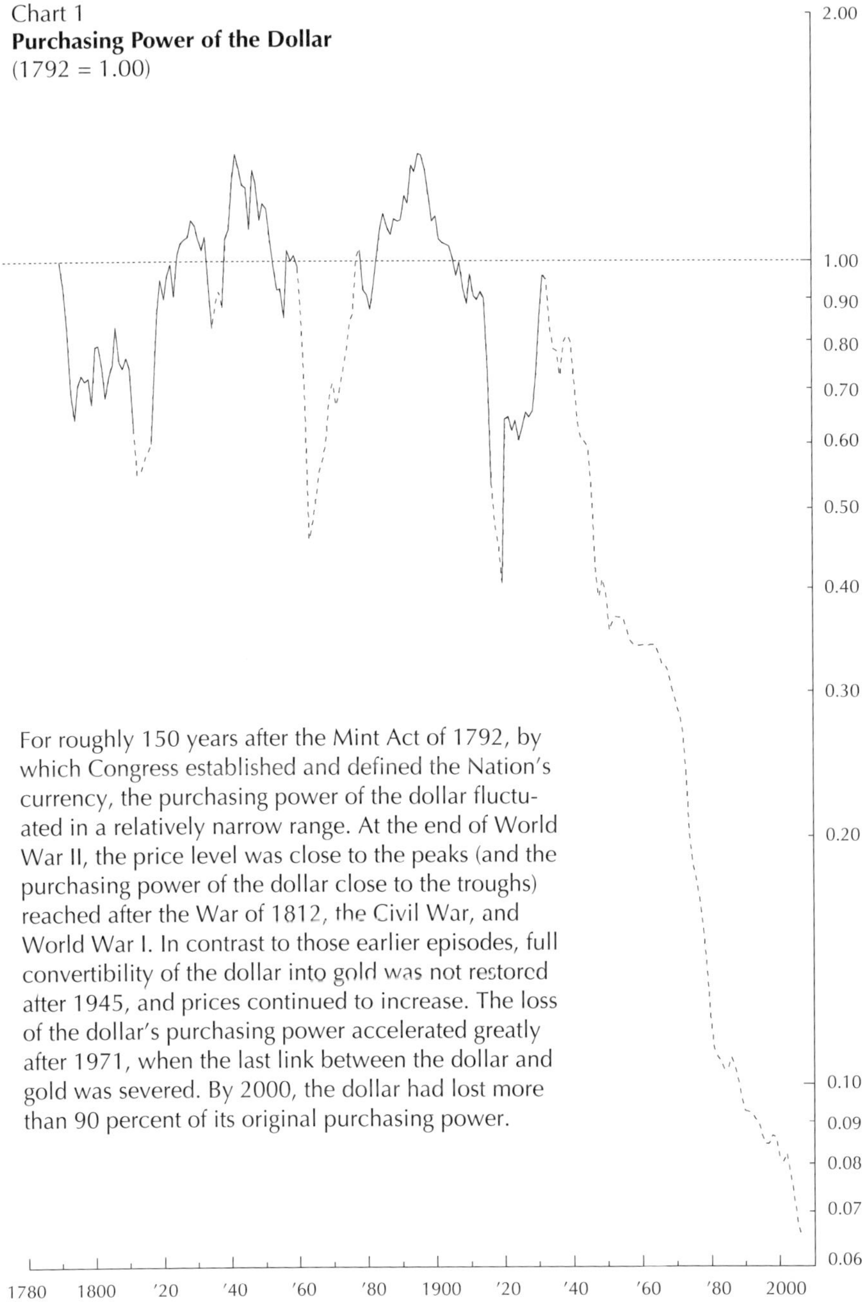

For roughly 150 years after the Mint Act of 1792, by which Congress established and defined the Nation's currency, the purchasing power of the dollar fluctuated in a relatively narrow range. At the end of World War II, the price level was close to the peaks (and the purchasing power of the dollar close to the troughs) reached after the War of 1812, the Civil War, and World War I. In contrast to those earlier episodes, full convertibility of the dollar into gold was not restored after 1945, and prices continued to increase. The loss of the dollar's purchasing power accelerated greatly after 1971, when the last link between the dollar and gold was severed. By 2000, the dollar had lost more than 90 percent of its original purchasing power.

Note: Purchasing power was calculated from the Wholesale Price Index (source: Bureau of Labor Statistics, U.S. Department of Labor). The broken portions of the curve are periods when redeemability of the dollar into the monetary commodities at fixed rates was suspended.

inflating and taxes meant that anyone who continuously rolled over T-bills for the 50 years actually *paid* the Treasury thirty three cents (1950 dollars) for the privilege of lending it one dollar!

Principal and Income

A corollary of the traditional notion that sound investing meant buying and holding high-grade, fixed-currency claims was that only the interest income from such holdings should be used to meet living expenses. The story is told of a female member of a proper Bostonian family who was picked up by the police for streetwalking. At the urgent family conference that followed, the head of the family asked:

> "Emily, how could you do such a thing?"
> "I needed the money," she calmly replied.
> "But your father took care of you in his will, why didn't you use that money?"
> "Why, that would be spending out of capital!"

The notion that spending principal is wrong, or at least shameful, would have been heartily endorsed by Mr. Forsyte. It was okay to spend the interest but "Never sell Consols." Chronic, officially sponsored inflating has changed this ancient principle of investing too, although it continues to be enshrined in trust indentures, and most outrageously in the tax code, which taxes as income the portion of interest received and realized capital gains that do

Chart 2
Value of $1.00 Invested in Treasury Bills

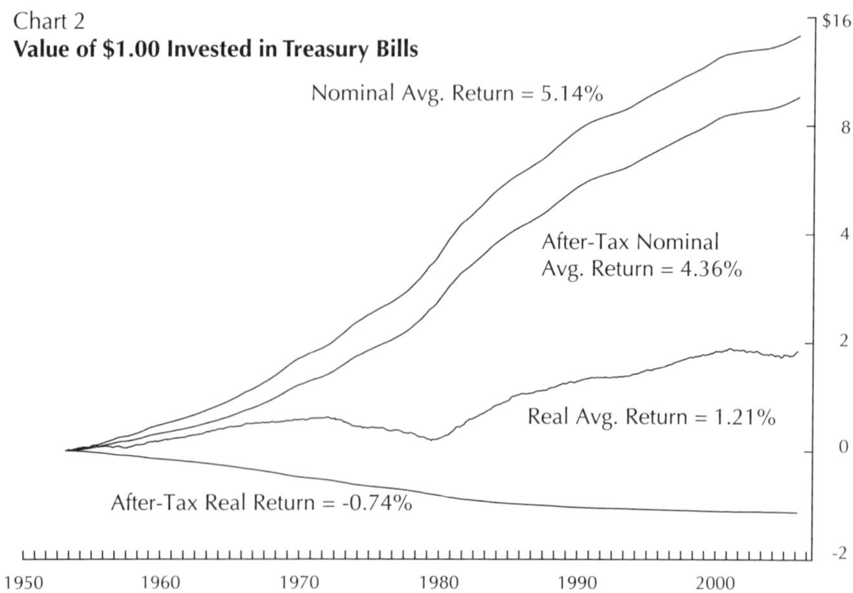

no more than offset the losses in purchasing power from the depreciation of the currency in which they are measured.

As mentioned above, interest rates can incorporate an inflation premium to compensate for the loss of the purchasing power of the principal. Similarly, higher asset prices may simply reflect general increases in the cost of living rather than genuine capital gains. From the individual investor's point of view, looking only at the nominal values of principal and interest can result in what can only be described as irrational, if not self-destructive, behavior.

Consider, for example, a retired couple who bought gold coins 35 years ago as a hedge against inflation, when the price of gold was less than $50 per ounce. They may now find themselves strapped for cash as price inflation has eroded the purchasing power of their sources of retirement income. Because they view the coins as capital, they may be reluctant to sell any to supplement their cash income even though that is precisely what they should be doing and the very reason that the coins were purchased in the first place.

On the other hand, some investors apparently view all interest receipts as spendable income. When price inflation abated from its most recent peaks, interest rates did too. The decrease in interest rates prompted many investors to seek higher yields by switching to riskier investments such as junk bonds even though the abatement of price inflation meant that their real incomes (after-tax income less the loss in the purchasing power of the principal) had changed little.

The point is not so much that such investors were ill-advised to hold fixed-dollar investments. Real income from these investments was in fact very little, if anything, both before and after interest rates and price inflation decreased. The point is that lower nominal rates accompanied by lower price inflation is not a sound reason to accept more risk.

Some Things Don't Change

Chronic inflating has not changed the fundamental importance of living within one's means as the key to becoming a successful investor. What is different is the accounting—determining what your means really are. In the first example given above, the retired couple failed to understand that gains on their gold coins had offset decreases in the purchasing power of their retirement income. Oppositely, spending all nominal interest as income is a surefire prescription for a progressive decrease in the real value of one's holdings.

More generally, there is no reason to believe that a regime of fiat currency has served to increase the long-term returns that can be expected from investment capital to more than their historical levels of four percent or less. Indeed, there is much reason to believe that even that level may be difficult to obtain if inflating accelerates.

As the foregoing discussion of holding Treasury bills illustrates, the real returns from holding risk-free dollar claims are likely to be very low, even negative. The fundamental dilemma facing investors during an age of fiat currencies and chronic inflating is that in order to receive an acceptable rate of return, one has to accept the possibility of losses. As the late Arthur Okun of the Brookings Institution, who served as the Chairman of President Kennedy's Council of Economic Advisors, put it:

> The opportunity of safe saving is lost in a period of sizable and unpredictable price increases. Some assets offer a degree of protection against inflation in the sense that their values are likely to move up as consumer prices rise. But no asset shows a good year-by-year correlation with prices; even corporate equities and real estate are not good anti-inflationary hedges by this test. They may actually tend to outpace the price level on the average in the long run, but only with wide swings and great uncertainty.
>
> Our financial system ought to serve both investors who want to earn maximum returns (and are willing to take substantial risks) and holders of reasonably safe assets who view their saving largely as deferred consumption. The latter are not accommodated during inflation...the unsophisticated saver who is merely preparing for the proverbial rainy day becomes a sucker.*

This perhaps is the greatest single affliction of fiat currency: it forces risk-averse investors to become speculators to one degree or another. The speculative elements become 1) what will the dollar be worth when my investment is sold or matures; 2) what will my investment be worth when it is sold or matures; and 3) how much of the nominal income from an investment will be taxed away?

Accepting Risk

Money has served three traditional functions: as medium of exchange, as standard of value, and as store of value. All governments of the world have embraced fiat currency and inflating, with the results evident in Chart 3. This means that, while their currencies can continue to serve the first function of money in transactions, their usefulness as standards of value are

* Arthur Okun, et.al., *Inflation: The Problems It Creates and the Policies It Requires,* New York University Press, 1970.

subject to the distortions of fluctuating foreign exchange rates, and most of all, currencies have become unreliable stores of value, especially over the long term.

Resolving the investor's dilemma means that, in order to achieve an acceptable real return in terms of purchasing power, today's investor must rely to a greater or lesser extent on holdings that can fluctuate markedly in *price*.

It is only by accepting the possibility of losses in terms of currency (as well as purchasing power) that investors can expect to mitigate the double whammy of price inflation and taxes.

Chart 3
Purchasing Power in the United States of Gold and Selected Currencies
(1913 = 1.0)

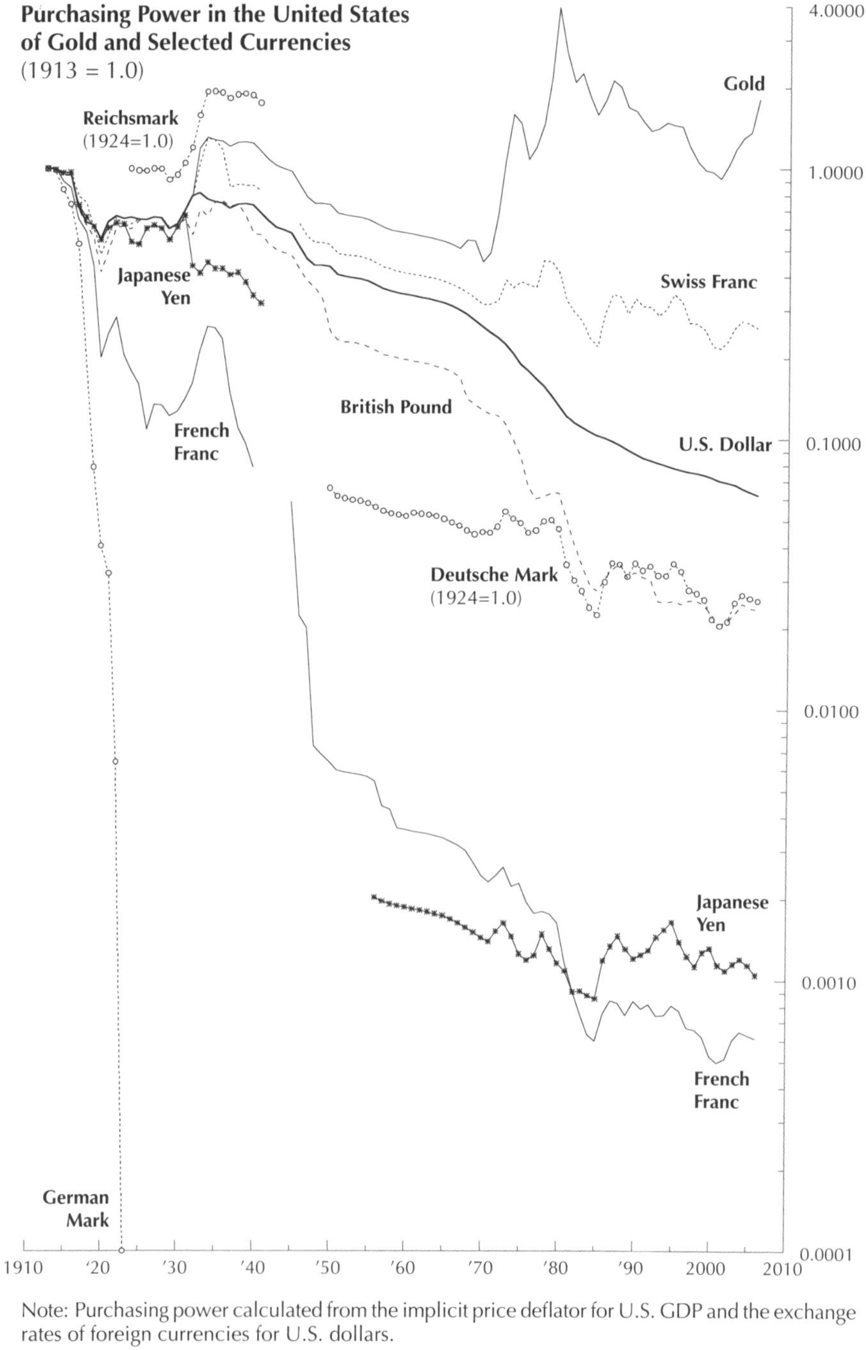

Note: Purchasing power calculated from the implicit price deflator for U.S. GDP and the exchange rates of foreign currencies for U.S. dollars.

III.
UNDERSTAND AND AVOID NEEDLESS COSTS

THE holdings needed to protect against the *purchasing power risk* that we discussed in the previous chapter will, to repeat, be subject to other risks. In Chapters IV and V, we discuss in some detail how to cope with *market risk*, which is simply the fact that the prices of investments can decrease as well as increase. However, we first need to describe one of the easily avoided hazards of investing—excessive costs.

There are armies of financial professionals who would like your business. These include stockbrokers, money managers, financial planners, and insurance salesmen. In addition, there are countless salesmen eager to sell you tangible items (everything from antiques to zircons) as good investments. These people are paid for their efforts in one way or another.

The costs of investing reduce the investor's return. They are one of the most easily overlooked obstacles to successful investing, yet they are perhaps the most readily controlled. There are essentially three kinds of investment expenses. Two of these are linked to purchase and sale transactions: commissions and spreads (the differences between the bid and asked prices that are available to the investor at any given time). Some investments involve ongoing expenses in the form of fees to a manager, storage costs, or similar outlays. These can vary widely, according to the type of investment, but they all reduce the investor's returns. Commissions and spreads tend to be high on tangible items which, with few exceptions, also require outlays for their storage and maintenance while you hold them.

Tangible Items

Whenever currency becomes unacceptable, readily interchangeable items (such as cigarettes or bottles of liquor) quickly emerge as exchange media. In addition, when a currency's value is destroyed, nearly anything of tangible worth can function as a store of value. For example, in the German hyperinflation of the 1920s, many families purchased household furnishings such as carpets, or even pianos, as a means of preserving value. We are a long way from conditions such as that, yet many tangible items are offered as "good investments." Such items include commemorative coins, plates, and other knick-knacks, as well as lots in yet-to-be developed vacation paradises and similar items sold with elaborate marketing campaigns.

Household tangibles, which have also become known as collectibles in recent years, usually require considerable care and maintenance, which will entail some expenditures of money or time for their owners. More significantly, unless you are prepared to become a dealer and to become highly knowledgeable about such items and the market conditions for them, *at any given time you can expect to pay roughly twice as much to buy as you can expect to receive from a sale of the same item.* Large spreads between bid and asked prices are typical even for things such as diamonds or numismatic coins that do not require much in the way of storage, care, and maintenance. In fact, the only tangible items of which we are aware that do not require much in the way of care to hold or expertise to buy and sell are newly minted or common-date, precious-metal coins. These trade at relatively narrow premiums over the intrinsic value of their metal content.

Some artworks or antiques have appreciated markedly in value over the years. For example, assuming Vincent van Gogh's painting *Irises* was worth less than $100 when it was painted, its annualized rate of appreciation over the 100 years before the J. Paul Getty Museum acquired it in 1990 for about $60 million may seem fabulous. However, that gain works out to about 15 percent per year. The chance that you own or will be offered anything equivalent to *Irises* must be reckoned as close to nil. More to the point, even if what you buy today proves to have artistic merit and value in the long run, given the bid and asked spreads on such items, in all likelihood it will have to appreciate considerably before you can gain anything by selling it. The commissions to high-end auction houses run upwards of 20 percent. Dealers acting on their own behalf might charge less, but more likely they would mark up their wares by more than that.

Real Estate

Real estate is widely regarded as an attractive investment and as an inflation hedge. With commissions and closing costs typically amounting to under 10 percent, the effective bid and asked spreads on real estate purchases and sales are reasonable. As mentioned above, personal residences are heavily favored by the tax code and other regulations. As a result, personal residences are most families' largest single investment and home ownership is nearly universal among those with higher incomes and larger net worth.

However, real estate as an investment (over and above a place to live) can be burdensome. Real estate is tangible and in the instance of land, "they have stopped making it." However, property taxes on undeveloped land can make it costly to hold. Developed properties, residential or commercial, generate income, but they require active management (dealing with tenants, repairmen, building inspectors, *et. al.*). Moreover, such holdings, unlike, say, gold coins that must ultimately be "prised out of one's cold, dead hand," may be vulnerable to arbitrary taxation and even confiscation. For example, laws and increasing regulations about lead paint, wetlands, hazardous wastes, etc., can make a property a time bomb that can go off on the unsuspecting or unaware investor.

Each parcel of real estate is unique and the expertise needed to buy, sell, and manage it is usually beyond the ability or desire of average investors. In any event, direct investment in and management of real estate is clearly beyond the scope of this booklet.

Real Estate Investment Trusts (REITs) that hold and manage income-producing properties on behalf of their stockholders can provide useful diversification for equity investors. Along with gold-mining company shares, the prices of REITs tend to fluctuate differently from those of other stocks and thus can provide useful diversification in a portfolio. In addition, to preserve their tax status, REITs must pay out substantially all their income to stockholders, which means that, in some circumstances, they can provide useful cash flows.

In general, with the exception of low-premium bullion gold coins and one's personal residence, directly held tangible items should not be considered to be or purchased as investments. Not only are transaction costs high, but also there may be ongoing expenses to be paid while they are held, and even if they are well-selected the returns may not be very large.

You should buy tangible items because you like them and expect to enjoy owning them. As investments they are likely to disappoint. If you are tempted to buy something only because you are being led to believe that it will appreciate, don't buy it.

While especially applicable to tangibles, this rule is applicable to all investing. In particular, when the person advising you of the appreciation potential of an item stands to receive a commission or other compensation for selling it to you, it is likely that the best thing to do is to just say no. A common attribute of poor investments seems to be that they are sold to, rather than purchased by, the investor, *i.e.*, the contact is initiated by the salesman hoping to sell something rather than by the investor looking to buy a particular kind of investment. Anything that the person selling you an investment receives in the transactions will reduce the value of your investment immediately, and it will diminish the eventual returns you will receive when the item is sold.

Securities

Securities (stocks and bonds) generally may be bought and sold with very low commission costs and with relatively narrow spreads between bid and asked prices, especially in comparison to tangible items. This does not mean that investors should not pay attention to the costs involved when investing in securities. Brokerage commissions can vary markedly among firms, and even among the customers of a given firm.

The commissions at full-service brokers can be 10 or more times what a discount broker would charge for the same transaction. Also, the quality of service at security-brokerage firms seems to vary far more among individual offices of the same firm, rather than among full-service or discount firms. The full-service brokers will chat with you about stocks and investments. However, brokers offering their services as money managers and who suggest you rely on their expert advice, while paying relatively high commissions, have a built-in conflict of interest. Their compensation depends on the amount of trading you do with them, which means that they will benefit from trades that may not be in your best interest.

Another reason to avoid the full-service firms is that their other services usually include underwriting (bringing new securities to market), and less commonly secondary distributions (selling large blocks to retail customers on behalf of the seller). In either instance the security will be offered at a set price with no commission charged. This means that the broker is being paid by the seller, typically somewhat more than the broker usually gets on transactions. When the broker has an Initial Public Offering (IPO) to sell, you are unlikely to get much if the subsequent trading is well above the offering price—brokers tend to dole out such shares to favored clients or to cheer up clients for whom they have lost money recently. But you can probably get all you want if the offering is a flop and quickly trades below the offering price.

Some full-service firms have attempted to avoid their central conflict-of-interest problem of being paid only when the client trades by offering "wrap accounts," in which the investor pays a flat annual fee and is not charged commissions on individual trades. Wrap fees typically run to two or three percent annually. This compares very unfavorably to the expenses of better mutual funds, even allowing for the fact that mutual funds do not include trading costs in their reported expense ratios (see below).

Discount firms do not try to sell you anything or give you advice—they just take your orders. This is not to say that discount firms always serve investors well. In particular, some firms have offered special facilities for individuals who are encouraged to become active traders with very low margin requirements on trades that are closed out in a single day. The problem is that though the commission on each trade may be very low, after many months of day trading their cumulative total may be greater than what the investor began with, which makes it very difficult if not impossible for the investor to make money.

Mutual Funds

Cost considerations apply to mutual funds as well. Trades in closed-end-fund shares, as well as the newer Exchange Traded Fund shares, are subject to brokerage commissions, the same as ordinary stocks. Open-end funds, which sell and redeem shares according to their Net Asset Value (or NAV, which is the total value of a fund's assets divided by the number of shares in the fund), often have loads, which translate into a lower bid than asked price at any given time. These are usually justified as paying for the marketing of the fund's shares. No-load funds are sold and redeemed at the same price at any given time, but some include marketing costs (reported as 12b-1 fees) in their annual expenses.

Some open-end funds, especially those that specialize in relatively illiquid securities, charge a redemption fee by redeeming shares for slightly less than their NAV. Even though redemption fees have the same effect as loads, they are not the same, because the redemption fee is retained in the fund, and, strictly speaking, such fees are not an expense to the investor. Rather, redemption fees are a recognition that, to meet redemptions, the fund may have to liquidate holdings that can depress the prices below the levels used to compute the fund's NAV.

All mutual funds have ongoing expenses, and these expenses reduce the returns to investors. Annual expenses include compensation for the managers and the people who keep books and audit them, as well as the costs of communicating with stockholders and complying with the securities laws. A fund's total annual expenses as a percent of its NAV is called the expense ratio. The average for all mutual funds is about 1.4 percent, but the expense ratio can be much higher or substantially lower. Once again, the more you pay in loads and expenses, the better the fund must do to provide you with a competitive return.

Mutual funds trade securities and thus incur additional expenses. However, these expenses may be implicit in the execution prices or explicit in brokerage commissions, and they may also reflect other services such as research. Thus, there is no standard way of reporting what mutual funds pay in trading costs. The best way to gauge what a mutual fund pays in trading expenses is its *turnover ratio*, which is half the total of its purchases and sales for a year divided by its NAV. A high turnover ratio for a fund presumably means that it is paying out relatively more in brokerage costs than a fund with a relatively low turnover.

Pay Attention to Costs

The point of this chapter is that acquiring and holding investments involves costs to the investor. Costs reduce returns, and they are far more predictable and stable than those returns. This means that investors should determine the costs of an investment, especially the up-front costs that immediately reduce the value a holding, before investing. Some costs must be stated explicitly to investors in an offering statement or prospectus. Other costs, particularly those related to the marketability of an investment once it is made (the difference between bid and asked prices) are seldom stated explicitly. Such differences can be exceptionally large for tangible items, but can also apply to certain kinds of securities, such as limited partnerships.

To repeat, an important principal is to avoid investments sold to you by salesmen who receive a portion of the price. Such items can include

How Exchange Traded Funds Work

The creation of an ETF begins with an *authorized participant*. These are highly scrutinized by ETF funds *managers* for integrity and operational competence. The authorized participant purchases or borrows the appropriate basket of securities and delivers them to a specially designated *custodial bank* for safekeeping. These baskets are normally quite large, equivalent to tens of thousands of shares of the ETF. The custodial bank then delivers shares in the ETF to the authorized participant.

The bank holds the basket of stocks in the fund's account for the fund manager to monitor. There isn't much activity in these accounts. Some cash is received as dividends and interest and paid out to the ETF's shareholders and for the manager's fee. Securities will be sold or purchased in the event of a change in the defined basket of securities.

The flow of individual stocks and ETF certificates goes through the Depository Trust Clearing Corp., the agency that records individual stock sales and keeps the official record of these transactions. It records an ETF transfer of title just like any stock. Once the authorized participant obtains the ETF from the custodial bank, it is free to sell it into the open market. From then on ETF shares are sold and resold freely among investors on the open market.

Redemption is simply the reverse. An authorized participant buys a large block of ETFs on the open market and sends it to the custodial bank and in return receives back an equivalent basket of individual securities which are then sold on the open market or returned, if they had been borrowed.

An ETF fund's manager receives a fee, a portion of which is paid to the custodial bank, paid from the fund's assets. These fees are typically very small. The lenders of securities, if any, used to make up a basket will receive a small interest fee, which will be paid by the authorized participant, who can profit by buying or selling when there is a sufficient difference in price between the basket of stocks and the ETF.

The process may seem complicated, but competition among authorized participants serves to keep the price at which an ETF trades close to the NAV of a share in a fund. One of the advantages of ETFs is that the creation and redemption of shares is a so-called *in-kind* trade of essentially equivalent items that does not trigger capital gains for investors. This means that, in contrast to an open-end fund, an investor will seldom incur a taxable capital gain (or loss) until he sell his ETF shares.

anything sold on the telephone or via direct mail and IPOs, or secondary distributions of equity securities. Brokers *sell* these, and if they are doing a good job for their clients, they are not putting your interests first. More generally, anything that sounds too good to be true probably is.

Brokers, Investment Advisers and Financial Planners

Some investment expenses are well worth their cost. It is very important, however, that you understand how much you are paying and what you are getting for your payment. Investment service providers offer different types of services subject to a variety of Federal and state regulations. These govern, among other things, whether the provider has a clear obligation to act in your best interest and/or disclose conflicts of interest.

Important distinctions—including whether the provider has a clear obligation to act in your best interests or disclose conflicts of interest—depend on which legal category the provider falls into under our securities laws. Securities laws recognize two types of providers—*investment advisers*, who are in the business of giving advice about securities, and *brokers*, who are in the business of buying and selling securities on behalf of customers.

Investment advisers are subject to a *fiduciary duty*. That means they are required to put your interests ahead of theirs at all times by providing advice and recommending investments that they view as being the best for you. Investment advisers are required to provide up-front disclosures about their qualifications, what services they provide, how they are compensated, possible conflicts of interest, and whether they have any record of disciplinary actions against them. They are regulated directly by either the U.S. Securities and Exchange Commission (SEC) or by state securities regulators. You can find out whether a person or firm is registered or licensed as an investment adviser by calling your state securities regulator, by using the contact information on the website www.nasaa.org, or by visiting www.adviserinfo.sec.gov.

Brokers are generally not considered to have a fiduciary duty to their customers. Brokers are only required 1) to know your financial situation well enough to understand your financial needs, and 2) to recommend investments that are suitable for you based on that knowledge. They are not required to provide the up-front disclosures required of investment advisers. In addition to being regulated directly by the SEC and by state securities regulators, brokers are subject to regulation by industry self-regulatory organizations, including the National Association of Securities Dealers (NASD) and the New York Stock Exchange. You can find out whether a person or firm is registered or licensed as a broker and check out their disciplinary record by calling your state securities regulator using the contact information on the NASAA website: www.nasaa.org or by visiting http://pdpi.nasdr.com/PDPI.

Financial planners are not separately regulated. Instead, their regulation and the level of responsibility they owe customers depend on the type of services they provide. Planners who provide investment advice must be registered or licensed as investment advisers and are subject to a fiduciary duty. Those who trade securities must be registered or licensed representatives of brokers. Some financial planners perform other activities that do not involve securities and therefore are not regulated under laws governing either investment advisers or brokers. The fact of the matter is that self-described financial planners who do not explicitly charge for their services are often little more than insurance or mutual fund salesmen who receive commissions when you purchase what they recommend. A qualified financial planner who is not encumbered by such conflicts of interest will charge by the hour.

The legal situation is further complicated by the fact that different standards can apply when investment providers serve as *both* investment advisers and brokers. For example, investment advisers who also buy and sell securities for customers must meet the requirements applicable to both investment advisers and brokers. The same is not true of brokers. They are permitted to offer investment advice in connection with their brokerage services without being regulated as investment advisers. As a result, the advice they offer is subject to the suitability standard that governs brokerage activities rather than the higher fiduciary duty that applies to investment advisers.

IV.
UNDERSTANDING RISK

ACCEPTING risk is, as discussed at the end of Chapter II, essential if an investor is to cope with the virtual certainty of continuing long-term debasement of the currency. In today's environment, placing one's savings in fixed-dollar claims will result in very low, even negative, returns in terms of purchasing power. When an asset is subject to risk, it means that the return from holding it will to a greater or lesser extent be determined by changes in its price (up or down), rather than by the income, if any, received while it is held.

As we discussed in the previous chapter, high transaction costs and the time and effort needed to become successful in buying and selling things (tangible collectibles, art works, etc.) or in managing directly held real estate means that such activities are better described as businesses rather than managing one's investments. The major exception is one's personal residence, because owner-occupancy is so heavily favored by the tax laws and other government policies. Above all, the major component of the return (a place to live) is not taxed as income. Another exception is gold coins that trade at low premiums over the intrinsic value of the metal they contain, where the major return is the ability to *have* some purchasing power in any circumstance, no matter how dire. (See the box on p. 34.)

What this means is that the only practical alternative to simply keeping one's money in the bank is to invest in securities—longer-term IOUs payable in currency as well as common stocks. Table 1 on pages 28-29 shows the annual rates of return on several major categories of securities for the years 1978-2006 (the three highest returns in a given year are shown in boldface type). The table also shows the average rate of return in each category over the 29 years, the standard deviation of those annual returns in each category (standard deviation is a measure of the average dispersion of returns; see box on p. 31), and the best and worst performance of each category over a 12-month span (*i.e.*, from the end of a month to the end of the month 12 months later, rather than the calendar years shown in the table).

We urge the reader to study Table 1 very carefully and to refer to it often while reading the remainder of this book. It reveals many aspects of investing in securities that are not widely understood or appreciated.

Most people and even market professionals tend to view stocks (typically as measured by a popular index such as the Dow Jones Industrial Average or the S&P 500) and interest rates (say, as offered on money market funds)

Table 1

Annual Percentage Returns on Selected Asset Classes, 1978-2006

(The three highest each year are in **Boldface**)

	Domestic Common Stocks							*International Stocks*		*Fixed Income*		
	S&P 500	*Large Cap. Growth*	*Large Cap. Value*	*Small Cap. Growth*	*Small Cap. Value*	*Gold Bullion*	*REITS*	*Large Cap.*	*Small Cap.*	*90-Day T-Bill*	*5-Year T-Notes*	*L-Term Gov't Bonds*
1978	6.6	7.0	3.7	17.5	22.0	**37.0**	11.0	**33.2**	**65.5**	7.2	3.5	-1.2
1979	18.4	16.5	23.0	**49.2**	38.3	**126.6**	**49.0**	2.1	-0.8	10.4	4.1	-1.2
1980	32.4	35.4	16.5	**52.4**	22.3	15.1	33.1	**38.5**	**35.5**	12.3	3.9	-4.0
1981	-4.9	-7.6	14.2	-10.9	**17.3**	-32.2	**17.9**	0.9	0.1	**16.5**	9.4	1.9
1982	21.4	21.7	**27.3**	19.4	**41.2**	14.2	20.9	5.2	0.0	13.1	29.1	**40.4**
1983	22.5	14.6	27.2	19.6	**48.1**	-16.8	**32.2**	22.2	**36.1**	9.3	7.4	0.7
1984	6.3	-0.7	**15.8**	-13.9	8.3	-18.7	**21.9**	11.4	11.6	11.1	14.0	**15.5**
1985	32.2	**32.5**	31.5	28.9	32.7	5.8	6.5	**48.1**	**67.5**	8.5	20.3	31.0
1986	18.5	14.7	21.3	2.4	14.2	19.6	19.7	**63.4**	**59.5**	6.8	15.1	**24.5**
1987	5.2	7.4	-2.2	-13.4	-6.1	**23.8**	-6.6	**42.3**	**40.7**	6.7	2.9	-2.7
1988	16.8	12.7	**25.8**	14.5	**30.7**	-15.2	17.5	25.0	**25.9**	6.9	6.1	9.7
1989	**31.5**	**36.2**	29.3	19.6	16.5	-2.8	2.7	14.4	**30.8**	9.0	13.3	18.1
1990	-3.1	1.1	-13.5	-18.7	-23.6	-3.1	-23.4	-18.9	-17.9	**8.4**	**9.7**	**6.2**
1991	30.5	**43.0**	27.6	**53.6**	**40.7**	-8.5	23.8	13.8	5.8	6.4	15.3	19.3
1992	7.6	6.3	**23.5**	4.6	**35.2**	-5.7	**15.1**	-9.8	-20.6	3.9	7.2	9.4
1993	10.1	0.9	22.3	10.6	**27.2**	17.7	15.1	**36.3**	**34.4**	3.2	11.2	18.2
1994	1.3	2.6	-5.7	-6.7	0.1	-2.2	2.7	**6.8**	**15.9**	**4.2**	-5.1	-7.8
1995	**37.6**	**37.8**	**36.6**	28.8	32.8	0.9	12.2	13.3	2.7	6.0	16.1	31.7
1996	**23.0**	**22.6**	14.7	9.3	24.1	-4.5	**37.0**	7.2	4.4	5.3	2.1	-0.9
1997	**33.4**	**30.6**	27.0	10.0	**38.4**	-21.7	19.7	-4.4	-16.9	5.4	8.4	15.9
1998	**28.6**	**39.5**	**20.3**	-1.5	-1.4	-0.5	-17.0	14.6	9.2	5.2	10.2	13.1
1999	21.0	26.8	-0.7	**46.6**	7.8	0.9	-2.6	**32.3**	**33.1**	4.8	-1.8	-9.0
2000	-9.1	-13.5	20.9	-23.4	22.1	-5.4	**31.0**	-16.3	-11.4	6.2	**12.6**	**21.5**
2001	-11.9	-14.6	-0.7	-0.1	**22.5**	0.7	**12.4**	-21.9	-17.8	4.4	**7.6**	3.7
2002	-22.1	-22.6	-25.1	-32.1	-9.1	**25.6**	3.6	-14.1	-3.7	1.8	**13.0**	**17.8**
2003	28.7	27.9	27.9	**54.7**	**64.1**	19.9	36.2	40.6	**60.9**	1.2	2.4	1.4
2004	10.9	7.5	20.1	15.1	21.4	4.7	**33.2**	**20.4**	**33.1**	1.3	3.2	9.3
2005	4.9	4.1	11.6	-0.7	9.1	**17.8**	14.0	**15.7**	**19.5**	3.1	1.4	7.8
2006	15.8	9.5	22.8	8.7	**22.9**	**23.9**	**36.1**	25.0	25.6	4.9	3.2	1.2

Summary Statistics for the Total Returns on Selected Asset Classes. 1978-2006

	Domestic Common Stocks							*International Stocks*		*Fixed Income*		
	S&P 500	*Large Cap. Growth*	*Large Cap. Value*	*Small Cap. Growth*	*Small Cap. Value*	*Gold Bullion*	*REITS*	*Large Cap.*	*Small Cap.*	*90-Day T-Bill*	*5-Year T-Notes*	*L-Term Gov't Bonds*
Annualized Return	13.22	12.5	15.0	9.5	19.9	4.8	15.2	13.5	15.5	6.6	8.3	9.4
Standard Deviation	15.32	17.4	14.6	23.6	18.6	28.0	16.6	21.3	25.9	3.6	7.1	12.4
Best 12-mos	+61.0	+66.3	+56.2	+101.6	+95.4	+179.4	62.4	+86.1	+114.6	+17.0	+23.7	+54.4
Worst 12-mos.	-26.6	-34.1	-32.9	-41.6	-29.9	-37.7	-28.7	-29.7	-29.5	1.0	-5.5	-17.1

Note: all return calculations assume re-investment of dividends and interest, but do not include transactions costs or taxes. **Domestic Common Stocks**, exclude foreign stocks traded on U.S. markets, investment companies, unit trusts, and shares of beneficial interest and are ranked by their market capitalizations. The **S&P 500** includes the 500 largest companies. The category **Large Cap** stocks include the largest 1,400 or so compan es, which account for about 90 percent of the total market's valuation. When these are ranked according to their ratios of book value to market value, the 30 percent (excluding issues with negative values) with the lowest ratios are deemed to be **Growth** stocks and the 30 percent with the highest values are deemed to be **Value** stocks. The 3,000 or so companies accounting for the bottom 10 percent of the total market's valuation are similarly divided into **Small Cap Growth** and **Small Cap Value** classifications. The returns on **Gold Bullion** are based prices at the end-of-month PM.fix in London. The Returns on **REITS** are based on the Wilshire Index of Equity Real Estate investment Trusts. **International Stocks** include only companies in developed markets, and are classified as **Large Cap** (top 90 percent of total market value) and **Small Cap** (bottom 10 percent).

During the years since 1945, domestic small stocks as defined above have outperformed large stocks by an average of about 2 percent per year. During the same period, value stocks have outperformed growth stocks by an average of 5 percent annually. Presumably these premium returns reflect perceptions of risk.

as either high or low.

The major lesson to take away from Table 1 is that price fluctuations are too complex to be measured by a single number. The returns on various segments of the market simply do not move in lock step. A second, more subtle, attribute of the data shown is that whether the return on a given type of security is among the highest or lowest returns during one year bears little or no relationship to its relative return in prior or in subsequent years—*there is no discernible pattern in the annual rankings of returns.*

Finally, it is essential to note that the return on a given type of security in any given year can differ from the average of all 29 years shown, especially over short periods. Nevertheless, long-term rates of return are related to the standard deviation of annual returns. High rates of return tend to be accompanied by a relatively high standard deviation of those returns.

Does Standard Deviation Equal Risk?

In studying investment returns, standard deviation indisputably is a measure of their volatility. Volatility, in turn, presumably is the manifestation of all the various risk factors involved in a given investment or type of investment. Because it is a purely mathematical calculation that produces a quantifiable result, the standard deviation of a set of returns on various types of investments (such as we have shown in Table 1) is a useful means of comparing the multitude of risks carried by various alternative investment opportunities.

The values for the average rates of return and the standard deviation of the returns shown in Table 1 are only for the years shown (annual returns for 1978-2006). Other starting or ending points, or using monthly or quarterly data, give somewhat different values. In general, changing the starting and ending dates is likely to have a larger impact on the evident rate of return than on the standard deviation of the monthly returns. The total return can vary a lot from period to period, but the volatility of a given class of investments changes little. Nevertheless, no matter what periods or classes of assets are reviewed, the general principal that above-average rates of returns tend to be accompanied by above-average volatility is nearly always evident.

That said, it should be noted that volatility of the returns on an investment is not in itself a complete measure of the probability of loss. As mentioned in the box on p. 31, the standard deviation of investment returns is measured from the mean (average) return. The underlying assumption is that investment returns are random and fall in a normal distribution around the mean. Standard deviation indicates the likelihood that the difference between a particular observation and the mean of all observations will be

Standard Deviation

Suppose you needed to know the average height of 10 people in a room. If 5 people were 6 feet, 1 inch tall, and the other 5 people were 5 feet, 11 inches tall, their average (mean) height would be 6 feet. Moreover, one might consider that average to be a good guess as to the height of any one of those people selected randomly from the 10 since all are within 1 inch of the mean.

However, suppose the height of a second group of 10 people was distributed as follows:

5 feet	2 people
5 feet 6 inches	2 people
5 feet 11 inches	1 person
7 feet	2 people
6 feet 6 inches	2 people
6 feet 1 inch	1 person

The mean height of the group again is 6 feet. However, the mean would be a poor estimate of the height of any one of the group selected randomly (*e.g.* a 7 footer could be selected).

Thus, the mean by itself can be a deceiving statistic—one can drown in a deep place in a river, even if the river's mean depth is 1 foot. What is needed is a measure of the *dispersion* of observations as well as their mean. The statistical tool commonly used for this is called the standard deviation, which in this case provides *a measure of the average dispersion of heights about the mean.* In the first case, the standard deviation is 1 inch. A person selected randomly would be expected to have an average height of 6 feet, plus or minus one inch. However, for the second group the standard deviation is 8.5 inches. Clearly the larger standard deviation provides confirmation that the mean is not as good an estimate of the height of any one person selected at random from the second group as it is of the first.

When there are only 10 observations the standard deviation might appear to be statistical overkill, since we can eyeball the data and notice intuitively that the mean is not as meaningful in the second group as it is in the first. For very large data sets, however, the dispersion of data is not as easy to gauge, so the standard deviation is a very valuable tool, since it allows us to gauge the dispersion of results at a glance.

For any set of data, the calculation of the standard deviation is a purely mathematical exercise. If the differences between the mean (average) of the data and each individual datum are randomly distributed around the mean, those differences will tend to exhibit a normal distribution. If the levels are plotted on the horizontal axis, and the frequency with which each level has occurred within the data set are plotted on the vertical axis, the familiar bell-shaped curve will emerge as more and more data points are plotted.

The mean value of a sample will be the center of the bell-shaped curve, and it will be an estimate of the mean value of all occurrences whatever is being measured. The standard deviation calculated from the sample provides an estimate of the extent of variation of all possible samples. Specifically, and again if the data are randomly distributed around the mean in a normal distribution, about two-thirds of all observations will fall within one standard deviation of the mean, and about 96 percent will fall within two standard deviations of the mean.

more than a given amount. Thus, if the average rate of return is 14 percent and the standard deviation is seven percent, there will be about a 1-in-6 chance that an observation will be less than seven percent (more than one standard deviation below the mean) and about a 1-in-50 chance that it will be less than zero (two standard deviations below the mean). In this example, there would also be a 1-in-6 chance that an observation will be more than 21 percent and a 1-in-50 chance that it will be more than 28 percent.

Consider, on the other hand, an investment that has a negative rate of return, say, a checking account from which the bank deducts a 1 percent service charge each month. This will decrease the account by about 5.4 percent per year, but the standard deviation of that rate of decrease will be zero. Thus, although it is risky to leave funds in a bank account subject to services charges in the sense that the account holder will suffer a loss, that loss is eminently predictable and the amount of funds available to be spent at any given time can be readily calculated with precision. (This is why funds for foreseeable outlays should be held in low-risk vehicles, despite their relatively low returns) Oppositely, the holder of an investment that is expected to return 15 percent per year with a standard deviation of 25 percentage points could only guess how much might be available for spending on some future date.

Fixed-Dollar Claims

Treasury securities provide perhaps the most straightforward application of the mean and its standard deviation to decision making.

Because they do not carry many of the often-discussed but difficult-to-quantify risks found in other types of securities (default risk, industry risk, etc.) and because purchasing-power risk pervades all investments equally (*i.e.*, from a U.S. investor's point of view, the ultimate payoff from any investment will be in spendable dollars, which will have the same purchasing power at any given time, no matter from whence they came), the differences in returns on various maturities of Treasury securities reflect only one factor—interest rate risk. Except during historically brief periods of extreme monetary stringency or financial panics, the prospective yields on Treasury securities increase with the length of time before they mature. This is because if interest rates increase before one's holding matures, it will trade for less than you paid for it. This possibility becomes greater when the maturity is farther in the future, and investors usually demand a premium over short-term rates if they are to "lock up" their funds for longer periods.

The average returns shown in Table 1 (based on annual data for 1968-2006) for six-month Treasury bills, 5-year Treasury notes, and long-term Treasury bonds were as follows:

	Bills	Notes	Bonds
Annual Return	6.6%	8.3%	9.4%
Standard Deviation	3.6	7.1	12.4

Using 81 years of monthly data for the years 1926-2006 gives the following results:

	Bills	Notes	Bonds
Annual Return	3.7 %	5.3%	5.4%
Annualized Standard Deviation	0.9	4.4	7.9

These data indicate the extent to which the average values of rates of return and their standard deviations are dependent on the particular data set that is used in their calculation. The longer period includes the years of the Great Depression as well as the overtly inflationary financing of the Second World War, when rates were very low.

However, the patterns of the data are consistent. That the average returns on Treasury bills are quite high in relation to their standard deviation indicates that returns of less than zero (*i.e.*, losses) can be expected to be few and far between for investors in Treasury bills.

That the standard deviations of the returns on 5-year Treasury notes and on long-term Treasury bonds are much larger in relation to their average returns suggests that losses are a relatively common experience for investors in those securities. In the instance of the long-term Treasury bonds, investors have experienced losses in roughly 1 year out of every 4.

As this is written, yields on Treasury bills, bonds, and notes are all in the vicinity of 5 percent (5.15 percent, 4.78 percent, and 4.87 percent, respectively). Although these are by no means the only maturities available, if you believe that interest rates are going to increase, then you should stay with the shortest maturities because higher interest rates will cause prices of longer maturities to decrease. On the other hand, if you believe that rates will decrease, at least in the near future, then you should be interested in longer-term issues. But what should you do if you are unsure?

The data show that, over the years, the increase in return from purchasing a long-term Treasury bond instead of a 5-year note has been small in relation to the increase in volatility of the returns. This is why those who are unsure of future interest rate trends should avoid not only the more volatile long-term issues, which will lose value if rates increase, but also short-term bills, that will, if rates decrease, have to be re-invested for a lower yield when they mature. In most circumstances, investing in fixed income securities with maturities of, say, three to seven years, can serve to limit both risks. Of course, when bills yield more than longer maturities (the current situation, which is unusual), short maturities are preferable until

Gold Coins

A collection of gold coins can form the cornerstone of any sound investment portfolio, but the reason to hold gold is not so much to make money as to *have* money in all circumstances. Investors without this security would be well-advised to begin a systematic program of accumulation of bullion coins, which are gold coins whose market value is directly related to their gold content and the price of gold bullion, with only a small premium over the intrinsic value (the weight of the gold content of the coin times the price of gold bullion). Such issues include the American Eagle, Canadian Maple Leaf, British Sovereign, Mexican 50-Peso, Austrian 100-Corona, and South African Krugerrand. The bid and asked spreads on such coins are very low, and, in contrast to holdings of bullion or gold bars, they can be purchased and sold without assay and in small amounts.

Coins may be purchased from a coin dealer, preferably one who is a member of the American Numismatic Association (ANA) or the more restrictive Professional Numismatists Guild. You may find a convenient coin source by checking the Yellow Pages of your local telephone directory and then consulting about any local coin dealerships with your local Better Business Bureau. Whenever possible, compare the prices being quoted by two or more dealers each time you make a coin purchase; this ensures that the actual price you pay is a competitive one.

The best prices can be obtained by purchasing round lots of coins (usually 20 coins per lot). You should also be advised that coin dealers are essentially salesmen, and they will often attempt to steer you to numismatic coins or to fractional ounce (1/4 oz., 1/2 oz. coins) of recent issue, where the dealer's margin is higher. These are to be avoided. You should stick to the full-ounce coins, the restrikes of various national mints, or to nonnumismatic condition common date coins originally issued as currency (such as British Sovereigns or U.S. Double Eagles).

Recent years have seen many bankruptcies among coin dealers. In making purchases from any coin dealer, no matter how reputable, simple prudence dictates that you arrange the transaction in such a way that you take possession of the coins *at the same time that payment is made*. This means that you should make the purchase in person, at the dealer's place of business. If that is not possible, you may arrange to use a bank as intermediary, with the bank not releasing funds to the dealer until the coins have been delivered. Once the coins are purchased, they should be stored in a readily accessible, but secure, storage facility, such as one or more safe-deposit boxes.

higher returns are available on the longer maturities.

In other words, to justify trading long-dated Treasuries one has to believe that future changes in interest rates and the prices of the long bonds will *not* occur in a neat, normal distribution of random fluctuations, but rather will reflect factors that can be analyzed and understood in advance. Needless to say it is a trivial matter to come up with an explanation of market movements *after* the fact; countless reporters and talking heads do so every day. To keep their jobs they do not even have to be correct!

V.
ACTIVE VS. PASSIVE INVESTING

THE Latin root of the word to speculate means "to see." A speculator is someone who presumes to see something that is not yet evident in the market price of the object of speculation.

Some hope to find clues to future stock prices by studying the patterns of past stock prices. Others pore over statistics and financial reports in hopes of forecasting economic trends and how they will affect stock prices in general or the fortunes of a given company in particular. Analysts, investment managers, and individual investors scrutinize such studies as well as corporate reports and filings with the Securities and Exchange Commission, and anything else that might be seen as an influence on the trends of market prices for securities, such as the weather or even sunspots.

Many newspapers, magazines, and newsletters are largely devoted to such topics, and some cable TV channels endlessly parade experts pronouncing on the latest news and developments, which are then chewed over in chat rooms and bulletin boards on the Internet. Brokerage firms, fund managers, investment advisors, and institutional and individual investors probably carry out the weightiest analyses, mainly for their own use. Such efforts are designed to facilitate what we will call "active investing," in which all purchases and sales reflect a belief that they have some knowledge that is not yet fully reflected in the prices of the securities to be bought or sold.

It should be borne in mind, however, that every recommendation from a broker or financial professional is an implicit assertion the current market price is not an accurate reflection of the prospective returns and risk of a potential investment, *i.e.*, that the market somehow has the price wrong. As a wag once observed, the three places in the world where it is believed that markets do not work are Cuba, North Korea, and Wall Street!

But what if prices, on average, do reflect potential returns and risks with some accuracy? What if all this activity by countless market participants does produce valuations that, again on average, more accurately reflect potential returns and risks than that of a single buyer or seller? If this is the situation, then prices will only change to reflect new or additional information, which will be inherently unpredictable. As a consequence, security prices will move in what statisticians call a "random walk"—that is, the most recent price quote is the best predictor of the next transaction and the next price change is completely independent of the previous price change.

This view is anathema to investment professionals. Clearly, they assert, some investments perform better than others; and, by determining the factors that account for these divergences, one should be able to select advantageous investments.

Given the infinite range of possibilities, some recommendations and predictions are bound to be successful in a given time period. Those whose picks do exceptionally well quickly acquire a following that drifts away once others begin to do better. But this is mainly a statistical phenomenon.

If 1,000 persons selected at random from a telephone directory were asked to name five companies whose stocks are attractive holdings for the year ahead (*i.e.*, whose stocks are underpriced relative to others), 12 months later there will be a wide dispersion of results among the 1,000 selections of five stocks each. Most will fall relatively close to average, but there will be a few outliers that have drastically underperformed or outperformed the average. There is little reason to believe that, at any one time, the current Wall Street superstars are benefiting from something other than this phenomenon.

The fact is that a majority of professional recommendations are mediocre. Many studies have concluded that selecting stocks by taping the stock market tables to a door and throwing darts will produce results that are equal or superior to following the buy lists of brokers and analysts.*

The Morningstar database (Morningstar, Inc., www.morningstar.com) lists 3,114 domestic common-stock mutual funds with 10-year performance records as of December 31, 2006, and a minimum initial purchase of $2,000 or less (*i.e.*, suitable for relatively small investors). The average performance of these funds over the 10 years ended December 31, 2006, was an annual return of 7.86 percent, which was 0.56 of a percentage point less than the performance (8.42 percent) of the S&P 500 index, which includes the 500 largest U.S. companies, during the same period.

Of these 3,114 funds, slightly fewer than 2 out of 5 (1,209 out of 3,114) did as well as or better than the S&P 500; more than 3 out of 5 (1,905) did worse. It should be noted that the total of 3,114 funds included only those funds that were in business for the entire 10 years—an unknown number of funds that were in business at the end of 1997 subsequently merged with other funds or ceased operations altogether, presumably because of

---

*Readers have occasionally questioned this assertion, inasmuch as *The Wall Street Journal* from time to time publishes a comparison of the performance of a few brokers' picks with that of stocks actually chosen by throwing darts at the stock tables. This often shows that the experts did better than the darts. What this article never mentions is that the potential rewards of success in this exercise—new customers and commission business—create a huge incentive for the brokers to shoot the moon. The brokers typically pick issues that are highly speculative and far more volatile than the average stock. If they come out on top, their phones will ring. Otherwise they haven't lost much.

poor performance.

Of the 3,114 there were 2,676 funds that charged front-end loads, deferred loads, and/or annual marketing fees (called 12b-1 fees, after the section of the SEC rules allowing for such charges). Their average annual load-adjusted performance* for the 10-year period was 7.77 percent, or 0.65 percentage points less than the S&P 500. Only 1,008 of these funds managed to better the S&P 500.

An obvious reason for the relatively poor performance of mutual funds relative to the S&P 500 is that indexes do not pay commissions, or loads. Nor do they have expenses, which averaged 1.50 percentage points per year for all 3,114 funds.

The remaining 438 "survivor" domestic common-stock funds with 10-year records did *not* charge marketing fees. Their average annual return for the period was 8.44 percent (slightly *more* than the S&P 500) with an average expense ratio of 1.16 percentage point, and nearly half (202 out of 438) of these funds managed to beat the S&P 500 during the past 10 years.

Mutual fund managers do not have to limit their holdings to companies included in the S&P 500. The total return on smaller U.S. companies during the past 10 years was over 11 percent. Had returns on the smaller companies simply matched the S&P 500, the funds' overall 10-year record presumably would have been worse than it was.

The point is that a mutual fund purchaser cannot reasonably expect to do better than the S&P 500 index unless he is willing to assume greater risks (more on this later).

In particular, many studies have shown that there is little reason to believe that a fund's relative performance in one period will be maintained in a subsequent period. As they say in the prospectuses, "past performance is not predictive of future performance." (The exceptions probably include funds that charge their shareholders exceptionally high loads and fees. These are very likely to continue to underperform less costly funds.) In other words, buying one of the 1,209 no-load funds that did better than the S&P 500 over the past 10 years does not give one a better-than-average chance of doing better than the S&P 500 over the next 10 years.

Index Funds

Included in the Morningstar database of domestic common-stock funds

---

* Load adjustments to the 10-year return spread the front or back-end load over a 10 year period. If the fund has been held for less than 10 years, the load would have an even larger impact on the total return.

are several dozen funds designed to track the S&P 500 index. Most of the differences in the returns in these funds are explained by differences in expenses. The lowest cost funds typically achieve returns that are close to the returns on the index.

There were about a dozen funds with 10-year records that tracked the S&P 500 and that were readily available to individual investors. The five best had an average performance for the 10 years ended December 31, 2006, of 8.20 percent per year, or 0.22 percent less than the S&P 500. The average expense ratio for the five funds was 0.38 percent. The leader was the Vanguard 500 Index Fund, with a 10-year performance of 8.34 percent. Not coincidentally its expense ratio was very low, only 0.18 percent.

Tracking an index is not quite as simple as it sounds. While shares of the companies in the index will comprise most of a fund's holdings, new cash coming in and paid out to redeem shares, as well as additions and deletions from the index, complicate matters. Most index fund managers use derivatives such as options and futures to keep the daily changes in their fund's NAV as close as possible to the changes in the index. This use of derivatives may not exactly compensate for the need to hold cash, which is why the difference between the return on a S&P 500 index fund and the index itself may not be equal to the fund's expense ratio.

A majority of those who purchased actively managed domestic common-stock mutual funds 10 years ago would have been better off had they purchased one of the S&P 500 funds instead. And we would expect that today an investor is equally likely to be better off buying and holding one of the easily purchased low-expense mutual funds tracking the S&P 500 index than buying one of the roughly 13,000 or so mutual funds that are managed by stock pickers.

Risk and Return

The fundamental reason for this lies in the nature of the relationship between risk and return. As discussed in the previous chapter, an investor can increase expected returns by assuming additional risk. However, assuming additional risk will *not necessarily* increase expected returns. To understand this, an analogy may be helpful.

One can cross a busy street at a crosswalk, a calculated but reasonable risk, with the expectation that he will be rewarded by getting to the other side. Alternatively one can blithely walk into the street at any spot without looking. The chances of arriving safely are considerably lower but the potential reward is no greater. Most pedestrians choose rationally to use the crosswalk.

The capital markets are similar; while higher returns are not obtainable without assuming greater risk, one can assume more risk without any expectation of earning a higher return. There is, if you will, "good risk" and "bad risk." We can identify the reckless risks and do away with them through careful and deliberate diversification. This leaves a portfolio exposed only to that risk which cannot be "diversified away." One can therefore *expect* to be compensated with higher returns in exchange for bearing this risk; this assumes that the historical performance of capital markets is a reasonable guide to the future.

To make this clear, it is first important to understand the distinction between different types of risk. *Company-specific risk* is the risk of investing in an individual company. There are random events that could occur—a lawsuit, a fire, the death of a key executive—that would primarily affect only that company. Indeed you could lose your entire investment in a stock if the news were dire enough to result in bankruptcy. *Industry-specific risk* is similar except that it refers to broader economic events that adversely affect an entire industry. Beginning in early 2000, for example, technology firms suffered declines far greater than the rest of the stock market. *Both types of risk are diversifiable*; by owning hundreds of stocks in many different industries, for every bit of "bad" news affecting a particular stock or industry, there would be an equal chance of offsetting "good" news emerging for another firm or industry in the portfolio. A well-diversified portfolio could be rendered worthless only by an economy-wide collapse.

Consider two hypothetical securities of comparable risk, stock A and stock B. If security A had higher expected returns than B, then investors would flock to security A and abandon security B; the price of A would rise accordingly and B would fall until the securities were priced at levels that produced equivalent expected returns. The market works toward an equilibrium in which all securities in a given asset class have the same expected returns. In this environment, an investor purchasing just one stock instead of the entire asset class would be unnecessarily assuming company and industry-specific risk. This would be irrational since he could purchase the entire asset class and garner the same expected return while dispensing with all of the risk attributable to that particular firm as well as the risk associated with its industry. Thus by choosing to invest in an individual company rather than in its entire asset class, one would be assuming risk that is uncompensated by additional expected return.

Modern portfolio theory posits that an investor cannot, however, dispose of the (non-diversifiable) risk associated with the entire stock market. This *market risk*, such as business-cycle fluctuations, is the risk common to all stocks. You can purchase an S&P 500 index fund, thereby eliminating all company and industry-specific risks associated with the firms held by the fund. However, you would still be subject to the fortunes of the broader stock market. So, once you have assembled an adequately diversified portfolio, you can increase your expected returns only by assuming greater market risk.

Subsequent research identified factors other than market risk that explained the returns to financial assets. Stocks could be categorized into asset classes defined by size and style (growth vs. value). Each of these asset classes (*e.g.*, small-cap value stocks) represents a potential stock portfolio that can provide investors with the opportunity to assume additional and unique forms of non-diversifiable (compensated) risk.

Note that we speak of the *expected* returns of asset classes. Just as there is no guarantee that the pedestrian, even when using the crosswalk, will cross the street safely, there is also no guarantee that an asset class, such as small-cap value stocks, will provide the investor with returns greater than the overall market, or even with positive returns. The investor may, for example, suddenly need funds for an unexpected calamity and be forced to "sell at the bottom" by liquidating his holdings amidst a bear market. Even the best-diversified portfolio cannot avoid these possible outcomes.

Up From Stock Picking

The approach we are suggesting is based on the notion that attempting to determine which stocks or industries will thrive, or which fund manager will have a "hot hand," is a fool's errand. Moreover, an actively managed fund may not follow a consistent investment strategy or policy. Fund managers who strive to pick "the best stocks" can change their minds. They also may attempt to "time the market" (adjust their holdings according to a forecast of broad trends). The managers themselves can change. What this means is that you may not be aware when a fund that has been purchased to serve a particular function in your portfolio is no longer serving that purpose because of a change in its approach or in its management.

Thus buying an S&P 500 index fund as a way of investing in domestic common stocks would be a move toward a passive investment strategy. To repeat, it is likely that a majority of common stock investors in U.S. common stocks would have done better if they had purchased an S&P 500 index fund instead of whatever they did.

The stocks in the S&P 500 index are, by definition, large-capitalization issues. As it happened, the 10 years that ended in 2006 was a period during which the S&P 500 underperformed, on average, the stocks of companies whose market capitalizations were too small to place them in the top 500. The index of the total market value of the next 2,500 companies returned

11.26 percent during the period. Passive investors need to find additional vehicles to participate in the wider market. But, before we discuss these, we should mention a further advantage of investing in index funds.

Tax Efficiency

Passive investing involves very low turnover, in contrast to actively managed portfolios which indulge in much more trading. Mutual funds must pay out in dividends any capital gains they realize. An active manager will sell an entire position in a stock simply to generate funds to purchase something else that seems more promising. In contrast, a passively managed fund will only sell a stock that ceases to meet the criteria for inclusion in the fund (*e.g.*, when a company is dropped from an index) or to meet redemptions. Even then, realized capital gains can be held to a minimum by identifying the lots that are sold. There are even passive funds that will "harvest" losses to offset any gains they are forced to realize. The returns on a "tax-managed" fund will be slightly less than its counterpart that is not so managed and therefore has lower turnover. Needless to say, this is irrelevant to non-taxable accounts, such as IRAs.

VI.
THE WIDER MARKET

THOUSANDS of times a day investors ask "how's the market doing?" The usual answer is that the market is up (or down) a number of points, which the questioner will understand as a reference to the change in the "Dow" (the Dow Jones Industrial Average, or DJIA) from the close of the previous trading session. While it may have many uses, the DJIA is an anachronism and it is statistically unsound.

When the Dow average was first calculated in 1896, it was simply the total of the prices of 12 different issues traded on the New York Stock Exchange (almost all of them railroads) divided by 12. This divisor was changed whenever there were changes on the list (additions, substitutions, stock splits, spin-offs, etc.). Recalculating the divisor ensured that the level of the average before and after a change would be equal. In 1928 the number of issues in the DJIA was increased to 30 (where it has remained ever since), but even then, because of numerous adjustments, the divisor was much less than 30 (16.7, in fact). The divisor is now 0.135.

The 30 issues included in the DJIA are selected by the editors of *The Wall Street Journal*, apparently on an *ad hoc* basis. The 30 issues are very large companies; together they account for about 20 percent of the total value of all 5,000 or so publicly traded stocks.

The way in which the DJIA is calculated reflects its beginnings in an era when there were no calculators or computers (and maybe not even adding machines). Its construction means that it is price weighted, which means that a percentage change in the highest price stock on the list will have a much larger impact on the average than the same percentage change in the lowest price stock on the list. Statistically, this is indefensible.

Nevertheless, the DJIA has tracked very closely with the Standard and Poor's index of 500 common stock prices (S&P 500), which is the series usually employed by serious students of financial and economic trends (and which is increasingly reported as a short answer to "how's the market doing?"). The S&P 500 (and nearly all other stock price *indexes*) is "cap weighted"—it is calculated from the total market capitalization (the market price of a stock times the number of shares outstanding) of domestic companies with the 500 largest market capitalizations. It is an index, rather than an average, and changes in the S&P 500 reflect changes in the total market value of the 500 largest stocks. Those 500 issues account for more than three-quarters of the total value of all domestic common stocks.

Other Indexes

Today, with nearly instantaneous communications and computers, more organizations than just Dow Jones and Standard and Poor's publish indexes of common stock prices, and those companies offer more indexes than they did just a few years ago. Many of these newer series are listed in the accompanying table. What they all have in common is that they are all calculated from the ranked market capitalizations of individual stocks.

Thus, it is possible to find an index for several ranges beginning with very largest market capitalization issue (currently Exxon Mobil, valued at nearly $400 billion) and continuing down the list to some stopping point. This point may be no. 300, 500, 1,000, 3,000 or even all the way down to the very smallest companies ranked at roughly no. 5,000, which have market values of a little over $1 million.

These organizations also publish indexes for intermediate ranges variously named "mid" "small" or "micro" capitalization stocks. It is important to understand that these categorizations are completely arbitrary and vary from organization to organization. For example, what Morgan Stanley International deems to be "Mid Cap" (nos. 301 to 750) falls entirely within the range that the Frank Russell Co. considers Large Cap (the Russell 1000).

The proliferation of indexes has led to a rapid increase in the number of index funds. Each such fund is designed to track a given index and may be either a traditional open-ended investment company or one of the newer exchange-traded funds.

As we discussed in the previous chapter, there are no valid before-the-fact reasons to expect that the portfolio holdings of an active manager will consistently out-perform or under-perform the stock market universe from which they are drawn. Specifically, there is no reason to believe that a fund or manager that "beats the index" in one period is likely to do so in a future period. The reason well over half of all investment portfolios (professionally managed or otherwise) fail to achieve the returns that indexes suggest they should, is that indexes do not pay management fees or incur trading costs—managers who charge high fees and indulge in heavy trading are even less likely to beat the indexes than managers who minimize their investors' costs.

Index funds have minimal costs and expenses. Their stock selections have been made for them, which means that they do not have to employ analysts and stock pickers. And they trade far less than actively managed funds, which can have turnover ratios* of 100 percent or more. An index

---

* The turnover ratio of a mutual fund is calculated as the gross proceeds from all sales divided

fund's turnover ratio seldom goes beyond single digits.

The rationale of index funds is the notion that common stock prices reflect all available information at any given time and that new information will come to light in a random fashion. In other words, on the assumption that markets work to price the prospective returns and risks of financial assets with accuracy (or at least more accurately than any one investor can with any consistency), efforts at stock picking are futile. Investors should concentrate on what they can control: expenses and risks. As we have noted, index funds are an excellent way to limit expenses when investing in equities. But how to control risk?

Diversify to Control Risk

Andrew Carnegie said "Put your eggs in one basket. And watch the basket. That is the way to make money." Few would recommend this as an investment strategy today, particularly for an investor who is not the principal owner and manager of a business (as Carnegie was). In fact the principle that diversification reduces risk may be the only thing about which all investment experts agree.

But does diversification reduce returns, as Carnegie apparently believed, and as the evident trade-off between volatility and total return would suggest? Clearly this is the situation when less volatile items with lower returns (such as Treasury securities) are substituted for a portion of a common stock portfolio. But what about a portfolio composed entirely of domestic common stocks?

Of course, for a lucky few who get in on a successful enterprise, such as Microsoft, early on, diversification reduces returns—funds invested in other stocks that did not do as well as Microsoft would have, in hindsight, been better placed in Microsoft. But the Microsofts of this world are very few and far between, and substantial fortunes have been dissipated in the search for them. Overall we would not be surprised if more money has been lost than has been made in stocks deemed to be "the next Microsoft" by people who have bought stock in a fast-growing company after its founders have sold some of their holdings in a public offering and it has become actively traded in the market.

As discussed in the preceding chapter, most investors would do better with *more* diversification of their common stock holdings. Passive investing is based on the belief that prices and interest rates are unpredictable and fluctuate randomly. The goal of the passive investor is to harvest the higher

---

by the total assets in the mutual fund. In plainer English, turnover represents how much of a mutual fund's holdings are changed over the course of a year through buying and selling.

returns that equities (common stocks) have provided over the years while limiting costs and risks as much as possible. Empirical studies demonstrate that risk and return are related over the long term. The volatility of returns is the usual measure of risk and, in general (but not always), higher long-term returns are associated with larger short-term volatility of those returns.

The proliferation of funds that track additional indexes has created opportunities for further diversification—what some have called "asset class investing." Some segments of the market have had higher long-term returns than the S&P 500—small stocks and value stocks in particular. The short-

Table 2
Selected Common Stock Price Indexes

Index	*Includes Stocks with Market Caps Ranked*			*Percent of Total Mkt. Cap*
Standard and Poor's				
500 (Large-Cap)	1	to	500	76.4%
400 (Mid-Cap)	501	to	900	11.1%
1000	501	to	1,500	16.0%
600 (Small-Cap)	901	to	1,500	4.9%
Composite	1	to	1,500	92.4%
Dow Jones				
Large-Cap	1	to	307	67.1%
Mid-Cap	308	to	855	17.8%
Small-Cap	856	to	1,623	8.4%
Total Market	1	to	1,623	93.3%
Frank Russell Co.				
Russell 1000	1	to	1,000	87.2%
Russell 2000	1,001	to	3,000	11.3%
Russell 3000	1	to	3,000	98.5%
Russell Microcap	3,001	to	4,000	1.2%
Small Cap Completeness	501	to	4,000	23.3%
Morgan Stanley Capital International				
Large-Cap	1	to	300	66.7%
Mid-Cap	301	to	750	16.3%
Prime	1	to	750	83.0%
Small-Cap	751	to	2,500	14.4%
Investable Market	1	to	2,500	97.4%
Micro	2,501	to	5,000	2.6%
Broad	1	to	5,000	100.0%
Wilshire				
5,000	1	to	5,000	100.0%
4,500	501	to	5,000	23.6%
Dimensional Fund Advisors				
Large (CRSP 1-5)	1	to	1,279	90.5%
Small (CRSP 6-10)	1,280	to	4,310	9.4%
Micro (CRSP 9-10)	1,806	to	4,310	4.0%

term volatility of the returns on those market segments is larger than it is for the S&P 500; but when they are included in an investment portfolio, to the extent that the fluctuations in their rates of returns are uncorrelated, the volatility of that portfolio's returns will be less than the average of its individual components.

In other words, the reason to include stocks not included in the S&P 500, is not only that other segments of the market have had higher returns, but to moderate volatility.

However, it should be understood that an index fund can only serve as an asset class within the context of a specific portfolio. For example, a portfolio of, say, 6 different actively-managed mutual funds would not, in fact, be well diversified, if all 6 funds were focused on large capitalization growth stocks. Similarly, an S&P 500 fund and a fund that tracked the Russell 1000 should not be considered as two different asset classes within a portfolio—the coefficient of correlation of the returns on the two indexes during the past 27 years was 0.996!*

Most of the indexes shown in Table 2 have been broken down by their compilers between "growth" and "value." Again, there is no commonly employed approach to this division. In general, the issues in a given index are ranked according to one or more financial ratios (such as market price to book value, or cash flow). The stocks with the highest ratios are deemed to be "growth stocks" while those with the lowest ratios are "value stocks."

With the exception of the Russell indexes, the total market values of issues deemed to be Growth and Value are approximately equal within each group (Large, Mid, and Small). How many companies are deemed to be "Large-Cap," "Mid-Cap," and "Small-Cap" can vary greatly, as is indicated in Table 2.

The original S&P 500 index funds have been joined by many other funds passively tracking these domestic and foreign indexes as well. Some of these are briefly described in Appendix B. Appendix B also provides information on funds that, while they to do not attempt to track any particular published index, buy, hold and sell stocks according to parameters set forth in advance. For example, Dimensional Fund Advisors (DFA) considers a universe of about 4,500 domestic common stocks traded on the New York Stock Exchange, the American Stock Exchange, and NASDAQ. Not all publicly traded issues are included in this universe. DFA excludes foreign stocks,

---

*The coefficient of correlation between two data series is a statistical measure of their interdependence. The value indicates the degree to which a change in one variable is matched by a change in another and it can range from -1 (completely inverse correlation) through zero (no correlation at all) to +1 (complete correlation).

investment companies (including Real Estate Investment Trusts and limited partnerships), recent initial public offerings, companies in bankruptcy or involved in mergers and tender offers and similar corporate actions, issues with fewer than four market makers, with limited operating histories, and those failing to meet listing requirements or having similar problems.

Approximately 1,400 companies with the largest market capitalizations, accounting for over 90 percent of the total value of their entire universe, are deemed by DFA to be large companies. The remaining companies account for the other 10 percent of total market value. The cutoff is a market capitalization of about $1.7 billion.

In managing their funds, DFA deems the 20 percent of the large companies, and the 25 percent of the small companies, with the lowest ratio of price to book value to be value stocks. In short, the funds they manage in this fashion, while not index funds, are passively managed—buy and sell decisions are determined by simple and predetermined parameters.

The High Yield Dow (HYD) strategy, discussed in Appendix A, also is a passive approach, even though it involves identifying a very small number of individual stocks for purchase and sale on a monthly basis. The HYD strategy relies entirely on simple and predetermined criteria. The HYD holdings at any given time would be considered domestic large-capitalization value stocks.

Nearly any market capitalization index fund, as well as stocks selected by the HYD strategy, and fixed-income securities (money market or bond funds) can be used as a building block in a passive investment portfolio. The only requirement is that the costs be as low as possible and that the investment characteristics should be immune to the whims of an active fund manager.

VII.
THE BUILDING BLOCKS

IN a passive investment portfolio, the commitment to equities should be divided among several asset classes. This will vary according to the investor's resources and situation. For example, a portfolio may not be large enough to include, as its large capitalization value stock component, the High Yield Dow stock selection strategy (see Appendix A) efficiently. Similarly, one's broker or one's employer-sponsored retirement plan may not have access to all the mutual funds you might wish to use, but may be able to provide acceptable alternatives.

The history of stock prices has been extensively studied for many years (the most extensive database is maintained by the Center for Research in Securities Prices at the University of Chicago). A major finding of this work is that there is a relationship between firm size (measured by market capitalization) and return. A second major finding is that there is also a relationship between returns and investment style, *i.e.*, stocks that are richly priced (presumably because their prospects are better than most) vs. those that are cheap. This distinction is usually expressed as growth vs. value. We believe that these labels obscure the characteristics of each group. We have adopted the growth and value names only because they have become widely accepted.

Ibbotson Associates defines large stocks as those with market capitalizations large enough to place them in the top half of all companies traded on the New York Stock Exchange ranked by market capitalization; small companies are defined as all the rest. Ibbotson further defines growth stocks as the 30 percent of issues with the highest ratio of price-to-book value and value stocks as the 30 percent with the lowest ratio of price-to-book value (the middle 40 percent is excluded).

Using these definitions of categories of domestic common stocks, Ibbotson calculated the following returns for the years 1927-2006:

	Annualized Return	*Standard Deviation*
All Stocks	10.2%	20.2
Large Growth	9.6%	20.3
Small Growth	9.1%	33.7
Large Value	12.5%	26.9
Small Value	15.6%	31.7

These categories comprise the major domestic common stock building blocks of a passive investment portfolio.

Why Not the Best?

The reader may well wonder why, given the historical performance of various categories of stocks, a long-term investor shouldn't simply buy the one that has performed the best? Over the 1927-2006 period of 80 years, small-capitalization value stocks outperformed the other three major categories of domestic common stocks by a wide margin, so why not put my money there and be done with it?

The answer to this question goes to the very heart of the passive approach to investing. First, as we have noted several times, annual rates of return can differ greatly depending on the period over which they are calculated. Moreover, the relative performance of the small-and-large, value-and-growth categories can vary greatly year-to-year. During the 1927-2006 period, small-capitalization value stocks were the best performing category in just 30 of the 80 years. On the other hand, small-capitalization growth stocks were the best performing category in 17 of those 80 years, even though they returned more than five percentage points less per year on average than the small-capitalization value stocks. Similarly, large-capitalization growth stock were the best-performing category in 18 of the 80 years vs. 15 years for the large-capitalization value stocks. Yet the value stocks outperformed the growth stocks by nearly 3 percentage points over the 80 years.

Thus, the reason not to purchase only small-capitalization value stocks (or any other single category) is that future returns in a portfolio will be calculated from present levels. Even if one is thoroughly convinced that small-capitalization value stocks will, if held long enough, emerge as the sector providing the highest returns, it could take many years to do so, and the expected volatility of those returns could be unacceptably high. Anyone deciding where to invest right now simply has no way of telling which category will do the best, not only during the next year, but for much longer periods.

By placing funds in several categories, the investor stands to beat the averages in two ways. First, rebalancing means that a portion of the holdings that have done better than the others will be sold to add to the holdings that have not done as well. By no means will every rebalancing trade be made at peaks and troughs of divergences (*i.e.*, recent trends of the categories may persist, so that delaying a given trade could enable the investor to sell higher or buy lower), but over the long-term, the returns on the various categories tend to be much closer to each other than in the short-term. Secondly, and especially when the returns on the selected categories are not highly correlated, holding several and rebalancing them in a disciplined way will serve to reduce the variability of the total returns on the entire portfolio.

When putting together one's own portfolio, the major components should be:

Large-Capitalization Value Stocks, which tend to have above-average returns with a below-average standard deviation. This category includes blue chips that are currently out of favor as well as companies in unglamorous industries or that are in some way distressed. The High Yield Dow stock selection strategy may be employed here, if resources permit. (The HYD strategy involves relatively frequent incremental trades, and attempting to follow it with less than roughly $100,000 can lead to unacceptably high trading costs or increased volatility.) Otherwise, funds that track the Dow Jones Large Cap. Value, the S&P 500 Value, or the Russell 1000 Value indexes should be used.

Large-Capitalization Growth Stocks, which include the current darlings of the investment professionals. Their price-earnings ratios tend to be high and their dividend yields tend to be low. Many passive investors may wish to give them less weight than large-capitalization value stocks, but they should not be omitted entirely—there are times when they do very well. If you are using the HYD strategy for your large-value stocks, then an S&P 500 index fund might well be used as your growth component because that index is dominated by growth stocks. Otherwise funds that track the Dow Jones Large Cap. Growth, S&P 500 or the Russell 1000 Growth indexes should be used.

Small-Capitalization Stocks, which tend to be more volatile than large capitalization stocks. These include the legions of "story stocks" that are heavily picked over by active managers and individual investors in search of the next Xerox or Cisco Systems. Although their high volatility can sometimes make them shine, their overall performance tends to lag the other categories considerably, as indicated above. Passive investors should only include small-capitalization *growth* stocks if they are held through a small-capitalization fund that does not specifically focus on either growth or value stocks, *i.e.*, funds that hold only small-capitalization growth stocks are probably best avoided.

On the other hand, as noted above, *Small-Cap Value Stocks* have been the best long-term performers and, despite their relative volatility, they belong in any passive-investment portfolio.

To our knowledge there are no mutual funds employing the Ibbotson criteria that were used to calculate the foregoing returns. Passive investors must choose from what is available. Given that the correlation of returns is lowest between the largest stocks and the smallest stocks, and that returns (and volatility) are higher for smaller stocks, investors should include the smallest-capitalization value stock fund available.

Brokerage firms and mutual fund management companies often create funds simply to have "new products." Many of these are not suitable for an asset-class investor. In general, industry-specific funds (those that hold, for example, only consumer product companies or only energy companies) are not useful asset classes. Exhaustive research has shown that the size and valuation (growth or value) of the companies within such funds account for most of the variation in their returns. *Real Estate Investment Trusts* (REITs), and *gold and gold mining companies* are two exceptions to this finding. *Foreign stocks* also tend to fluctuate differently from other equity investments. These three categories can provide additional building blocks in a passive investment portfolio. Their returns are less correlated to the domestic common stock categories shown above than those categories are to each other.

Gold and Gold Mining Companies

In our calculations of historical rates of return, we have used the bullion price. Gold bullion can be held directly in the form of gold coins, or indirectly via a mutual fund. Indirect ownership make a gold holding "just another piece of paper," which obviates one of the main reasons to own gold.

Shares in gold mining companies fluctuate with the gold price, but they are even more volatile. As far as we are aware, there is no long-term index of gold mining shares that assumes reinvestment of dividends, which is how all the other historical returns in the book have been calculated. Moreover the mining companies themselves have undergone many changes, not only with respect to where they operate, but also as a result of mergers and other corporate reorganizations. There are mutual funds specializing in precious metals, but none are designed to track any specific index (*i.e.*, they are all actively managed), and a large and variable portion of their holdings tend to be speculative or "junior" gold mines as well as silver, platinum, and even base metal mines, whose output is mainly used for industrial purposes rather than as a store of value, and whose profits tend to fluctuate with business conditions.

Accordingly, those wanting to participate in this sector should purchase shares in the few gold mining companies meeting the criteria that we believe make them suitable for investors as opposed to speculators. The first, and most important, criterion is that a company actually be producing. Secondly, the company must have adequate reserves to support production for a prolonged period. Thirdly, the company must not be overly leveraged, either financially through insupportable debt on its balance sheet or operationally via high production costs. Fourthly, a company must be large enough so that its shares are highly liquid and its operation adequately diversified to protect investors from political and other risks to company assets. Lastly, the company should pay a dividend so that investors can gain some current income from this portion of their portfolios.

That there have been periods of low and even negative investment returns associated with gold during recent decades and the fact that gold-mining share prices are volatile are not reasons to rule out participation in this sector. The very low correlations of the returns on gold-mining shares with those of other sectors means that rebalancing transactions will tend to sell some gold shares when they have increased in price and *vice versa*.

However, the decision to include gold bullion and/or gold stocks will also depend on the investor's view of the outlook. Specifically, how much longer will central banks, which still hold a very large proportion of the world's stock of tradable gold, continue to be net sellers, especially whenever the price of gold firms up? At some point the central bankers are likely to decide that their gold holdings, which are their only liquid monetary asset that cannot default, are no longer excessive. We would guess that level to be significantly more than zero, but we can only guess. Meanwhile, the world's stock of tradable gold is increasing by no more than one or two percent per year, which is far less that the rates at which fiat money is being created. This will lead to a much higher gold price at some future date, but again we can only guess how much higher or when.

The Useless Middle

As the discussion of the composition of various indexes in Chapter VI has indicated, what constitutes a "mid-cap" stock is in the eye of the beholder. Using extensive records of common stock prices developed by the University of Chicago's Center for Research in Securities Prices (CRSP), we examined the returns on the largest quintile, the smallest quintile and the middle 3 quintiles of U.S. common stocks ranked by market capitalization.

For the years 1926-2006, the median difference between the annual returns on the largest quintile and the smallest quintile was about 12 percentage points. During 74 of those 81 years, the returns on the 3 middle quintiles were somewhere between those on the largest and smallest quintiles. During the other 7 years, when the return on the middle quitiles was higher (or lower) than the returns on either the largest or smallest quintiles, the median difference from the closer of the two was about 2 percentage points.

Thus there is little reason to hold a "mid-cap" fund if the portfolio contains funds holding issues further down the list of companies ranked by size. To repeat, asset class investing takes advantage of dissimilar price movements.

Of course, to limit risk, a "mid-cap" fund could replace a fund that held smaller, but more volatile, companies.

A type of passively managed fund to be avoided is one based on "fundamental indexing." Such funds are based on standard indexes, but the weighting of the individual stocks is done on some criterion other than market capitalization. One way this has been done is to add up the total dividends paid by all the companies in an index, and weight each holding in the fund according to a company's dividends as a proportion of the total. This could also be done using reported earnings or cash flows.

Studies have shown that such procedures have produced better returns than a capitalization-weighted portfolio based on the same indexes. There is little reason, however, to believe that such returns reflect anything other than the superior returns on value stocks. The expenses of fundamental index funds are relatively high and they have more frequent trades. We believe that there are more efficient and less costly ways to "tilt" a portfolio toward value and away from growth.

A passive investment portfolio should cover many, if not all, segments of the market, but there is no set formula to follow. This brings us to the question of how passive the approach we are recommending really is.

The Active Part of Passive Investing

Selecting the components, and their proportions, in your portfolio will reflect the opportunities open to you, your appraisal of your situation and tolerance for risk, and your appraisal of the economic and financial outlook. This begins with the most basic decision of all—how to divide your holdings between equities and fixed-dollar claims.

For some investors, the notion that common stocks will generate higher returns in the long-term, while supported by the historical record, may take too long to be validated. There was a 20-year period, 1929 through 1948, when the total return on 5-year Treasury notes was higher than that on domestic common stocks, and there was a similar 16-year period between 1966 and 1982.

By the same token, if you believe that the widening acceptance of free markets around the world will continue, your commitments to foreign equities should probably include an emerging-markets index fund. But more cautious investors should probably stick with funds that concentrate only in Europe or, for the somewhat more adventurous, Europe, Australia, and the Far East (EAFE).

Similarly, if you truly believe in the "new economy" and expect that high-tech and dot-com stocks will resume their winning ways before long, then you probably will want a relatively large proportion of large-capitalization growth stocks in your portfolio.

In short, how an individual sets up his or her own passive portfolio will inescapably reflect personal opinions and biases. It cannot be emphasized too strongly that, as long as the holdings are well diversified among asset classes and whether or not your specific opinions prove to be correct will be much less important to your results than your ability and determination to stick with the program you set out for yourself. Changes in your allocations by sector should be made only because your circumstances have changed, not because of anyone's guess regarding the outlook for short-term returns on the various asset classes, or because you have developed new opinions regarding the long-term outlook. In turn, these opinions should reflect some very fundamental change and most emphatically not simply that one sector has gone up and you don't want to sell any of it or another has gone down and you do not want to buy any more.

The power of passive investing is that it can help you overcome the emotions that appear to govern the decisions of most investors: fear and greed.

Similarly, even though it is likely that stocks will provide better long-term returns than fixed-dollar claims, investors would be well advised to keep a portion of their holdings in fixed claims. By doing so, the volatility of one's holding will be reduced to acceptable levels, and a reserve will be available to purchase more equities if their prices decrease. In general it is sounder policy to adjust the expected volatility of one's portfolio with fixed-dollar claims instead of avoiding asset classes with above-average volatility of returns.

What's Right for You?

How an individual investor builds a portfolio will, to repeat, depend on the resources and opportunities available. Although we have indicated that a passive investment portfolio should hold several of the building blocks mentioned above, there is no need to hold them all or to give them equal weight. When building your own portfolio, you will have to select from the index funds that are available to you.

VIII.
BUILDING A PORTFOLIO

AS mentioned in the preceding chapters, failure to better the performance of the S&P 500 is the experience of the large majority of individual investors and fund managers. The issues included in the S&P 500 predominate in their holdings. Most would be better off holding all the issues in the 500, rather than attempting to out-guess the market when selecting a smaller number of stocks.

If, at the end of 1971, an investor had purchased an S&P 500 fund, (in Table 3 we call this Portfolio #1), his total annualized return for the 36 years through the end of 2006 would have been 11.3 percent and he would now have (before taxes) $4,214 for every $100 originally invested. The standard deviation of those annual returns would have been 15.1 percentage points.

The S&P 500 is dominated by large capitalization growth stocks. In Portfolio #2, we have added other sectors of the market, so that the S&P 500 index fund accounts for only one-third, with large and small capitalization value stocks (companies with low ratios of price to book value) accounting for the other two-thirds. The latter asset classes did better than the S&P 500 from the end of 1971 to the end of 2006 and, as might be expected, this change markedly increased the total return for the period by 3.7 percentage points over the S&P 500, but the standard deviation was only 0.5 percentage point higher.

In going beyond the S&P 500 we did not include small-capitalization growth stocks (relatively small but richly-priced companies, mainly traded on NASDAQ or in the "pink sheets"). Typically, the prices of these stocks have been bid up because they have been touted as having the potential for rapid and profitable growth, or even as the "next Microsoft." In other words, they are the most speculative category of common stocks. Although they occasionally do very well (see Table 1), among the four major classes of domestic common stocks (large, small, growth, and value) they have had the lowest long-term returns with the highest standard deviation.

Both large and small capitalization international stocks did better than the S&P 500 during the period. Large-capitalization foreign stocks did slightly worse than domestic large-capitalization value stocks, and small-capitalization foreign stocks did slightly better than domestic small-capitalization stocks. Portfolio #3 adds these two international asset classes to Portfolio #2, making their total equal to each of the three domestic asset classes. This increased the total return by another 0.4

Table 3

Building a Passive Portfolio

Portfolio Components (asset classes)	Percentage Allocation of Six Hypothetical Portfolios (#1) S&P 500 Index	(#2) Add Large & Small Value	(#3) Add Large & Small International	(#4) Add 10% Gold	(#5) With 20% Fixed Income	(#6) With 40% Fixed Income	Components Annualized Return 1972-2006	Components Standard Deviation
S&P 500 Index	100.0%	33.4%	25.0%	22.5%	18.0%	13.5%	11.4%	15.1
US Large Cap. Value	-	33.3%	25.0%	22.5%	18.0%	13.5%	14.5%	15.2
US Small Cap. Value	-	33.3%	25.0%	22.5%	18.0%	13.5%	18.5%	18.2
International Large Cap.	-	-	12.5%	11.3%	9.0%	6.8%	13.2%	18.1
International Small Cap.	-	-	12.5%	11.2%	9.0%	6.7%	16.2%	17.5
Gold bullion	-	-	-	10.0%	8.0%	6.0%	8.0%	21.0
5 Year T-Notes	-	-	-	-	20.0%	40.0%	7.9%	5.7
Total	100.0%	100.0%	100.0%	100.0%	100.0%	100.0%		
Returns for1972-2006 assuming annual re-balancing.								
Annualized Return	11.4	15.1	15.5	15.3	14.0	12.6		
Change from S&P 500	-	3.7	4.1	3.9	2.6	1.2		
Annualized Std. Deviation	15.1	15.1	14.0	12.8	10.5	8.4		
Change from S&P 500	-	0.0	-1.2	-2.3	-4.6	-6.7		
Growth of $100	$4,214	$13,464	$15,174	$14,286	$9,565	$6,192		
Best 12-mos. Span	61%	70%	61%	57%	51%	44%		
Worst 12-mos. Span	-39%	-31%	-33%	-25%	-20%	-15%		

percentage point, to 4.1 percentage points higher than the S&P 500 for the period, but brought the standard deviation down to 1.2 percentage points less than the S&P 500.

Portfolio #4 adds 10 percent gold bullion, with the remainder held in the proportions of Portfolio #3. Given that gold had a relatively low annualized return over the 35-year period (8.0 percent) and a very high standard deviation (21.0 percentage points), it may come as a surprise that the inclusion of 10 percent gold markedly reduced the standard deviation of the annual returns to 2.3 percentage points less than the S&P 500. As might be expected, holding 10 percent gold did reduce the annualized return, but only by very little—about 0.2 of a percentage point.

Adding fixed-income securities to one's holdings is the traditional way to reduce risk. Portfolios #5 and #6 include 5-year Treasury Notes (see pp. 32-36) in the proportions of 20 and 40 percent respectively. The balance of these portfolios is held in the proportions of Portfolio #4. As might be expected, adding fixed-income securities reduced both the returns and the standard deviations of those returns, but in both instances by much less than the weighted averages of the returns and standard deviations of the individual components. This is similar to what happened as additional asset classes were added to the S&P 500 in Portfolios #2 through #4. Here is a summary of those changes:

	Weighted —Avg. of Components—		—Calculated Results—	
	Annualized Returns	*Standard Deviation*	*Annualized Returns*	*Standard Deviation*
S&P 500	11.3	17.5	11.4	15.1
Portfolio #2	14.2	19.8	15.1	15.1
Portfolio #3	14.2	22.0	15.5	14.0
Portfolio #4	13.6	22.9	15.3	12.8
Portfolio #5	12.6	19.7	14.0	10.5
Portfolio #6	11.0	14.5	12.6	8.4

The 60-40 ratio of Portfolio #6 is considered the standard institutional or "endowment" mix of equities and bonds. Please note that the annualized return on Portfolio #6 for the 1972-2006 period is 1.2 percentage points larger than that for the S&P 500, while the standard deviation of the returns on #6 is 6.7 percentage points lower!

The reason for these seemingly miraculous results (higher returns with less volatility or risk) is that the annual returns to the various asset classes are not closely correlated. The coefficient of correlation between two data series is a statistical measure of their interdependence. The value indicates how much of a change in one variable is explained by a change in another. For the years 1972-2006 the coefficients of correlation of the asset classes used in these portfolios were:

	S&P 500 Index	Large Cap. Value	Small Cap. Value	—International— Large Cap.	Small Cap.	Gold Bullion	5-Year T-Notes
S&P 500 Index	1.00						
Large Cap. Value	0.81	1.00					
Small Cap. Value	0.64	0.82	1.00				
Int'l Large Cap.	0.57	0.46	0.36	1.00			
Int'l Small Cap.	0.38	0.28	0.28	0.92	1.00		
Gold bullion	-0.28	-0.33	-0.28	-0.09	0.01	1.00	
5 Year T-Notes	0.22	0.36	0.22	-0.07	-0.16	-0.21	1.00

The amount of expected volatility that is appropriate will vary from one investor to another. But whatever their needs and responsibilities or their tolerance for risk, all investors should attempt to deploy their assets in such a way that they cannot increase their overall expected returns without increasing their risk. Stated another way, they should not be able to reduce the risks associated with their holdings without reducing the expected returns.

Estimates of expected returns and their volatility (risk) are perforce based on historical experience. Needless to say, actual performance going forward will almost certainly be different. Over the long term, however, it is reasonable to expect that the *relative* risks and returns of various *asset classes* (in contrast to individual securities) will conform to historical experience.

Why Rebalancing is Important

Rebalancing each year means selling enough of the components that did better than the portfolio as a whole to bring them back down to the percentage selected when the portfolio was started, and using the proceeds to bring the other components up to that percentage. When the correlation of the components is relatively low, more often than not rebalancing will mean that most trades will be selling high and buying low—the presumed goal of every investor—and the process will augment the overall returns, as is evident in portfolios #2 through #6, described above.

Even though the correlations of the 5-year Treasury Notes with the stock components are quite low, adding the fixed-income component reduced the portfolios' returns and their volatility by more nearly equal amounts than adding value stocks, foreign stocks and gold. It would appear that this was because equities did well during the period under review, so that 26 of the 36 annual rebalancings involved selling equities to add to the lower-yielding fixed-income holdings. Had there been more instances of selling Treasuries to buy depressed stocks, adding the fixed-income component probably would have made the reduction of expected returns smaller and the reduction in the variability of those returns larger.

A buy-and-hold approach means that the better performing (and generally more volatile) components will become a larger proportion of the portfolio as time goes on. Rebalancing, while it can serve to enhance returns, serves mainly to keep a portfolio's volatility to the expected and tolerable levels. This is of major importance because most investors have a greatly exaggerated view of their tolerance for risk.

The fact of the matter is that most individuals tend to overstate their tolerance for risk. The effect of adding portfolio components to reduce volatility and risk is perhaps more evident in the best and worst 12-month spans shown at the bottom of Table 3. How large a setback could you be comfortable with? Could you really experience a set back of 25 percent or more, without panicking and losing sight of your plans and long-term goals?

IX.
WHY MOST INVESTORS FAIL

THE goal of investors and speculators alike is to buy cheap and and sell dear, but few do this with any consistency. This is so even for investment professionals, as we have noted many times. The common-stock investments of the overwhelming majority of mutual funds, pension funds, bank trust accounts, and investment advisors fail to achieve the returns indicated by the popular stock indexes. By the law of averages, some may do spectacularly well in any given year (and these are often flooded with so much new money to invest that they don't know what to do with it), but very few manage to beat the market over long periods.

Skating to Where the Puck Was

Individual investors often do far worse, buying into the very peaks of a market fad, and selling out (or being sold out) after the inevitable crash. They buy the stock of manufacturers of pin-spotting machines right before the last bowling alley is built. They sink funds into oil-drilling programs in marginal areas (remember the "overthrust" belt?) at the peak of petroleum prices.

They chase after new issues and obscure companies with a story (typically some new technological wonder) in hopes of "getting in on the ground floor." If such a company does manage to do well, they will bid its price up to fantastic levels, only to ride it all the way down when the euphoria ends. One sports-minded observer has described the strategy of the average investor as "skating to where the puck was."

It is usual to attribute this phenomenon to the conflicting human emotions of fear and greed. When people (including the professionals, who are, after all, human beings too) see others benefiting from an upward market move, they are prompted to get in on it too (greed). This process can often propel the prices of the object of speculation to previously unimaginable highs. The upward trend continues until the last buyer has been suckered in. When the inevitable crash comes, fear then drives the market and prices decrease sharply until the last speculator is flushed out, often at prices not only far below what was paid, but also well below any reasonable standards of worth.

As an aspect of human behavior, the tides of speculative price movements and manias have long been well described* but they remain little understood. In particular, no one has ever come up with a way of predicting

* One of the most useful studies was one of the earliest: *Extraordinary Popular Delusions and the Madness of Crowds*, written by Charles MacKay in 1841. This classic is still in print.

the duration of a particular mania or to what highs or lows a mania will propel prices.

Investors thus need to be constantly on guard against falling in with the crowd and succumbing to the conflicting emotions of fear and greed, the main reason investors become their own worst enemies. The investment approach we advocate in this book can accomplish much in this regard.

Limiting oneself to index funds holding hundreds or even thousands of stocks, or to the mundane stocks that typically turn up in the HYD strategy, will not give you much to brag about at cocktail parties. But it will enable you to avoid the ruinous love affairs that so many investors seem to develop with their favorite stocks.

More importantly, our approach should enable you to overcome perhaps the most basic impulse of investors, which is to want to have more of whatever has gone up and less of what has gone down. This is the impulse that presumably contributes to the manias and speculative peaks, and troughs, mentioned above. But, the punch bowl always runs dry just when the party is getting good, to paraphrase William McC. Martin. By selling into rallies and buying into declines, you will miss much of the euphoria, but you will suffer far less when the inevitable reaction occurs.

Reasonable Expectations

But there is another important factor in investment success: reasonable expectations. As Richard Russell* has written:

> ...the *wealthy investor never feels pressured to "make money" in the market...*
>
> The wealthy investor tends to be an expert on values.... And if there are no outstanding values, the wealthy investor *waits*. He can afford to wait. He has money coming in daily, weekly, monthly. In other words, he doesn't NEED the market. He knows what he's looking for, and he doesn't mind waiting weeks, months or years (they call that patience).
>
> What about the little guy? This fellow always feels pressured to "make money," to "force the market to do something for him." The little guy doesn't understand...compounding, and he doesn't understand money.
>
> ...He's impatient, and he constantly feels pressured. He tells him-

---

* The publisher of the biweekly *Dow Theory Letters,* available for $250 per year from P. O. Box 1759, La Jolla, CA 92038.

self he has to make money fast. And he dreams of "big bucks." In the end, the little guy wastes his money in the market, he loses his money on gambling, he dribbles it away on senseless schemes. In brief, this "money nerd" spends his life running up the down-escalator.

> Now here's the ironic part of it. If, from the beginning, the little guy had adopted a strict policy of never spending more than his income, if he had taken that extra income and compounded it in safe, income-producing securities—in due time he'd have money coming in daily, weekly, and monthly just like the rich guy. And, in due time he'd start acting and thinking like the rich guy. In short, the little guy would become a financial winner instead of a loser.

This is, of course, simply another statement of the principles we set forth in the Introduction and Chapter I. First and foremost, the key to becoming a successful investor is living within one's means.

The continuing depreciation of the purchasing power of the dollar can distort investors' perceptions, however. In particular, a prudent investor nowadays cannot, without diminishing its purchasing power, expect a portfolio to provide more real spendable income than the three to four percent of the principal's value that conservative bond investors received when currency values were stable. In an age of chronic inflating and taxation of nominal capital gains, even that level of returns may be difficult to match.

For individuals who depend on investment income for living expenses, the issue can become crucial if they wish to preserve their purchasing power and pass on the principal to their heirs. Because much interest income is not income at all but compensation for the diminished purchasing power of the principal, and because capital gains may be simply inflationary illusions, investors may come to believe that their financial position has improved when it has in fact deteriorated.

A possible solution for such investors would be to follow the procedures now used for the endowment funds of many nonprofit organizations: keep a running total or moving average of the value of your investment assets and withdraw a fixed percentage each year, without regard to the nominal income received.

For example, if the average value of your investments over the past five years is $120,000, it could be deemed prudent to withdraw four percent this year ($4,800 or $400 per month, an amount that it will be your goal to increase as time goes by). Retired persons might choose to withdraw a larger percentage, but only in the recognition that by so doing they could be spending some of the principal, as is the situation with an annuity.*

On the other hand, this is not a problem in tax-deferred pension accounts or where funds are to be accumulated without distinction between principal and income, where simply keeping their value ahead of general price inflation is a daunting but reasonable goal.

Acting Like an Expert

Richard Russell is mainly a student of market timing—a version of active management in the belief that the market can be beaten with sufficient study and understanding of current trends, based on analyses of the available information. We question this view. In particular his assertion that "the wealthy investor tends to be an expert on values" may appear quite intimidating as it seems to suggest that it is something one is born with, like 20/20 vision or perfect pitch. Some people may have an intuitive flair for making sound investment decisions, but clearly most people do not.

However, by building a portfolio that includes a broad range of asset classes and staying with it in a disciplined manner, anyone can make the market itself tell him or her what to do. All that is required is the time, the discipline and the effort to make it do so.

---

* Fixed-income annuities are the traditional means of financing retirement incomes. They pay more than other fixed-dollar claims because they are lifetime contracts—no value is retained for your heirs. See AIER's book *How to Build Wealth with Tax-Sheltered Investments* for more information on annuities.

APPENDIX A

THE HIGH YIELD DOW STOCK SELECTION STRATEGY

WE were intrigued by reports of studies indicating that investing in the highest-yielding stocks included in the Dow Jones Average of 30 Industrial Stocks (DJIA) produced consistently superior results, but we questioned the rigor of those we came across. Some of the methodological questions include whether the transactions and yield calculations were based on the current list of stocks, or on the list as it stood at the time decisions would have been made, and what rules for trading were assumed (*e.g.*, how often the list is reviewed, whether or not holdings are to be equalized by dollar amounts periodically, and how buyouts and spin-offs are dealt with).

Accordingly, since 1989 we have conducted our own studies of the returns from investing in the highest-yielding Dow stocks. We believe our research has been far more extensive than most. We did confirm the major finding of others who had investigated HYD strategies: that investing in the highest-yielding issues in the DJIA tended to generate higher total returns than the Average itself. We believe, however, our procedures to be unique in that:

- we examined the total returns to HYD strategies on the basis of hypothetical portfolios constructed on the basis of information that was available at the time (the DJIA list, prices and indicated dividend rates), rather than basing our results on year-over-year price changes and dividend payments;
- the portfolios were reviewed and updated monthly, using mid-month prices, plus or minus $0.125 per share to allow for trading costs;
- instead of only looking at 12-month intervals, we examined holding periods ranging from one to 36 months—each month the issues that qualified were purchased in equal dollar amounts and held (with any spin-offs) for the full holding period—each month the net positions accumulated over the preceding holding period were evaluated;
- we examined portfolios composed of just the single highest yielding issue through all 30 on the list.

Our studies indicated that the returns could be enhanced further by investing in fewer than 10 issues, and by holding them for longer than 12 months.

We calculated the results of all possible combinations: from holding the single highest yielding Dow issue for one month (*i.e.*, if it ranks number two or higher in the month after purchase or later, sell it and buy the new number one issue) to holding all the Dow issues for 36 months, with portfolio

Chart 4: **Total Returns on Fully Invested Portfolios from December 1963 to December 2006**

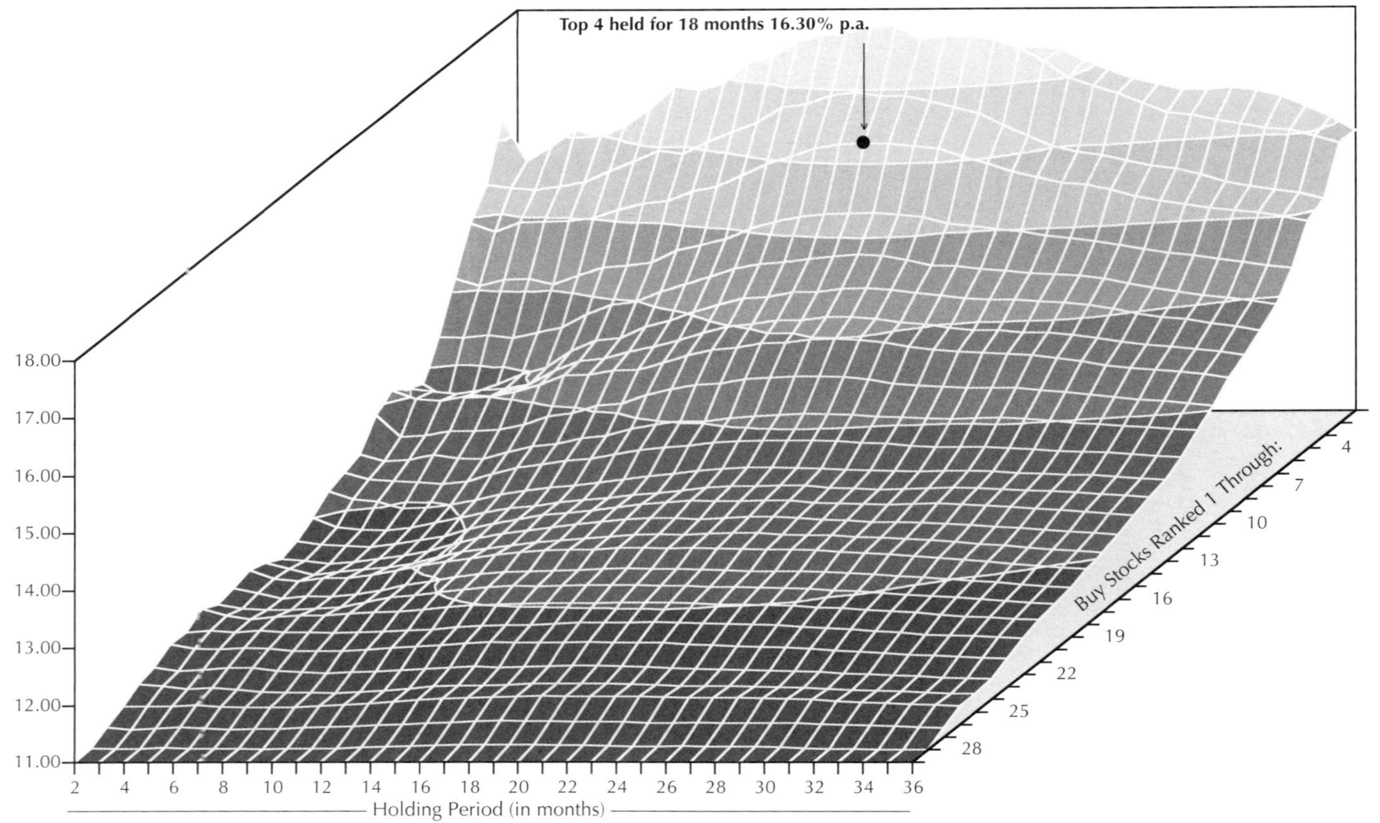

changes only reflecting reinvestment of dividends, splits, spin-offs and the deletion and replacement of issues in the DJIA.

The results of our study for the 43 years ended in December 2006 are shown in Chart 4. We found that purchasing the 4 highest-yielding Dow

Table 4: **Annual Percentage Total Returns on Large Capitalization Value Stock Indexes and on the High Yield Dow Strategy**
(1979-2006)

	S&P 500 Value Index	*Russell 1000 Value Index*	*Fama-French Large Cap Value Index*	*High Yield Dow Strategy*
1979	21.2	20.5	**23.0**	14.1
1980	23.6	24.4	16.5	**25.1**
1981	0.0	1.3	**14.2**	9.6
1982	21.0	20.0	**27.3**	11.4
1983	28.9	28.3	27.2	**38.0**
1984	10.5	10.1	**15.8**	15.0
1985	29.7	31.5	31.5	**32.0**
1986	21.7	20.0	21.3	**39.4**
1987	3.7	0.5	-2.2	**8.2**
1988	21.7	23.2	**25.8**	22.9
1989	26.1	25.2	29.3	**29.9**
1990	-6.9	-8.1	-13.5	**-3.9**
1991	22.6	24.6	27.6	**50.1**
1992	10.5	13.8	**23.5**	16.8
1993	18.6	18.1	22.3	**26.5**
1994	-0.6	-2.0	-5.7	**0.4**
1995	37.0	38.4	36.6	**43.0**
1996	22.0	21.7	14.7	**28.9**
1997	30.0	**35.2**	27.0	32.2
1998	14.7	15.7	**20.3**	11.6
1999	**12.7**	7.4	-0.7	-13.3
2000	6.1	7.0	20.9	**46.4**
2001	-11.7	-5.6	-0.7	**-0.1**
2002	-20.9	-15.5	-25.1	**-3.5**
2003	**31.8**	30.0	27.9	19.1
2004	15.7	16.5	**20.1**	11.5
2005	5.6	7.0	**11.6**	4.0
2006	20.8	22.2	22.8	**37.5**
Annualized Return	14.0	14.6	15.4	**18.6**
Standard Deviation	13.9	13.6	14.7	16.7
Best 12-mos.	60.8%	61.1%	56.3%	68.8%
Worst 12-mos.	-26.2%	-22.8%	-32.9%	-24.8%

stocks each month and holding them (and any spin-off attributable to shares purchased in a given month) for 18 months produced the most favorable combination of risk (volatility) and return over the 42 years ended in 2006.

Over the past 43 years, this approach would have provided an annualized total return about 6.0 percentage points more than what an investor would have earned by simply holding the Dow.

This is quite remarkable. The annualized return on the top 4-for-18 months (16.3 percent) is so much higher than that on the DJIA (10.2 percent) that, with all dividends reinvested, an HYD portfolio would become nearly 10 times as large as a DJIA portfolio that was the same size 42 years ago. Also, bear in mind that only a minority of portfolio managers and mutual funds do better than the stock market averages in a given year, and the proportion who manage to do so over extended periods is minuscule indeed.

There is, of course, no guarantee that such a high-dividend yield strategy will accomplish in the future what it would have in the past. The phenomenon that it attempts to exploit is that investments are subject to fads and fashions and, within the staid universe of the DJIA stocks, a company may become popular or unpopular for reasons that have little to do with its fundamental long-term condition and situation. These behemoth corporations tend to follow conservative and stable dividend policies, and unwarranted fluctuations in investor sentiment are then reflected in their dividend yields.

Our wholly-owned investment advisory firm, American Investment Services, Inc. (AIS) publishes the latest composition of the top 4-for-18 months High Yield Dow strategy each month in its newsletter, ***Investment Guide.*** AIS also manages individual and institutional accounts using this approach. In Table 4 we compare the performance of the 4-for-18 HYD strategy with that of two major "value" indexes that are tracked by mutual funds. These results, of course, are before expenses. Because it follows predetermined criteria for purchases and sales, the HYD approach is a passive strategy, even though it does not track any index.

A Passive Approach

This focus on current yields ignores most sources of stock market advice and information. The strategy, in effect, relies on the conclusions and findings (as evidenced by their actions rather than words) of only three groups of people: the editors of *The Wall Street Journal*, who pick major well-established corporations for inclusion in the DJIA; the directors and managements of the companies themselves, who set the dividend payout; and the investing public, who determine the price of the stock. The first two must be considered as more knowledgeable than the third. The editors do not select flash-in-the-pan enterprises for their index, and directors and managers generally do not declare dividends that their companies cannot afford or sustain.

On the other hand, it is the erroneous fashions and foibles of the investing public, including the herd of so-called professionals, that the strategy is attempting to exploit. In other words, the goal of the conservative common-stock investor should be to invest in solid businesses that are undervalued in the marketplace for one reason or another. Fads are most manifest in the brokerage reports, security analyses, rumors, and tips that most investors seem to rely upon in selecting stocks.

Another way of looking at it is that the superior performance of the higher-yielding issues in the DJIA is simply another manifestation of the market at work. If the distressed "smokestack" companies that typically offer higher dividend yields are in fact riskier than the high-flying growth stocks that dominate the other end of the list, then it should not be a surprise that the high-yielders provide higher total returns. Greater risk *should* provide greater returns.

The point we should emphasize here is that the HYD strategy is consistent with the approach we have outlined in Chapter V. Although it is not an indexing strategy, it most certainly is not a conventional "stock picking" approach. It is a passive, virtually mechanical approach in which we deliberately *ignore* the information (financial statements, products, management changes, competition, etc.) that is usually cited when making buy or sell recommendations. We believe such information to be reflected in share prices. The HYD approach is a way of investing in the very large companies that are in some way distressed and therefore more risky than the solid growth companies at the other end of the list of DJIA stocks ranked by dividend yield.

Why Just the Dow Jones Industrials?

The Dow stocks are chosen by the editors of *The Wall Street Journal*, apparently on an *ad hoc* basis, and as such they are an arbitrary selection of U.S. common stocks. Changes in the list are relatively infrequent and have often been forced upon the editors when an issue ceased trading because of mergers or buyouts. In general, the Dow stocks are those of well-known and very large companies. Most of the companies are household names, and it is clear that the Dow stocks are widely held, traded and followed—surprises and bizarre financial developments should be few and far between.

No doubt there are many excellent investment opportunities in nonindustrial areas. However, examining the levels of the broad averages (such as those published by the NYSE, S&P, or Dow Jones itself) reveals that the averages for the specialized industries are, without exception, markedly lower than the comparable industrial series. Presumably, this reflects the fact that sectors such as transportation, utilities, and finance are heavily regulated, and one goal of such regulation is to limit profits and investment returns.

Drawing one's stock selections from a larger list would necessitate holding many more issues, as many as 100 or more, to be comparable to the DJIA-based selection described above. This would be impractical for all but the largest portfolios. Also, if the selection were to be taken from, say, the top 25 dividend-yielding stocks of, say, the S&P Industrials, it would be likely that one's holdings at any given time would be more heavily concentrated in a given industry. An essentially arbitrary list, the Dow includes only one or two companies in a particular type of business.

More significantly, the top stocks ranked by dividend yield in a larger universe would be far more likely to include companies whose managements, for one reason or another, have not yet faced up to grave problems by cutting or omitting dividends. Focusing on the DJIA stocks means that investments in poorly managed, cyclical, and secondary companies will be minimized.

When a position is sold within a portfolio following a HYD strategy, it is usually because its price has increased relative to its dividend. Occasionally, it does happen that an issue will be sold because the dividend has been reduced or omitted. Sometimes this means that the position will be sold at a loss, but in other instances, a dividend cut is perceived as evidence that management is forcefully facing up to problems, prompting investors to bid up the stock's price.

Stable Dividend Policies are the Key

The key to the phenomenon that we are attempting to exploit is that the directors and managers of the companies in the DJIA, as well as most other large, publicly held U.S. corporations, follow a policy of paying regular quarterly dividends. Payouts are only increased when the insiders believe that they can be sustained for the long term, and they are only cut *in extremis*. This means that the quarterly dividend is an indicator of informed opinion on the long-term prospects of a company.

This is not the practice in most of the rest of the world. Even the largest European corporations, for example, typically declare annual dividends according to the year's results. If they have a good year, they pay a good dividend, and if they have a bad year, they do not. In this respect, the erratic dividend record of General Motors resembles its foreign competitors' record and for this reason we have excluded it from the calculations summarized in Chart 4 and Table 4. GM's dividend yield has not been a useful indicator for trading GM stock.

If what we might call the "European" dividend policy became widely followed among the DJIA companies, the selection strategy probably would not work as intended. There is no sign of this happening, however.

The insiders are under no obligation to declare regular dividends, but their attitude seems to be that their stockholders are mainly widows and orphans, whose major concern is a steady source of income. The dividend policies of smaller and most privately-held companies are far more contingent on short-term results—if it was a good year, then the dividend will be good, but if it was a bad year the dividend will be reduced or omitted completely. This is how corporations operated when they were invented, and it continues to be the usual practice for even very large companies in other countries.

Indeed, many students of finance believe that stable dividend policies are inefficient, because stockholders would be better served if managers paid out everything over and above what they can reinvest in their companies at an expected return that is higher than what the stockholder could receive on an alternative. There is little evidence that this view has received much acceptance in the United States.

Where there are large controlling stockholders, their tax situation has usually made it more attractive for them to have the company buy back its stock than increase dividends. Such purchases are typically for a limited time and limited amount. Buybacks are usually announced when large companies have excess funds on hand and management believes the market price of the company's stock is undervalued. As such they do not represent a long-term commitment, in contrast to an increase in the quarterly dividend. The second incentive against paying out cash when a company has a good year is that it is in the interest of managers and directors to enlarge the assets under their control, which can have a direct effect on their salaries and fees.

During recent years there have been an exceptional number of dividend cuts among the Dow stocks. Dividends have been reduced or eliminated when extraordinary factors have rendered previous levels impossible to sustain. Such factors have included sudden, adverse court judgments, as well as long-term changes in the structure of industries. In the latter regard, the editors of *The Wall Street Journal*, who select the companies in the DJIA, might be faulted for staying too long with poorly managed, burned-out companies. Nevertheless, there is little reason to believe that the increase in the number of dividend cuts reflects a changed attitude among managers and directors, *i.e.*, there is no evidence of a systematic trend toward setting dividends to reflect short-term or cyclical results.

What About Growth Stocks?

Much of the enormous expenditures of the securities industry on analysis and research is devoted to identifying growth stocks (shares in companies whose sales and earnings are increasing faster than most). Reputable brokerage firms will usually recommend buying and holding established growth stocks to conservatively oriented long-term investors.

One of the characteristics of growth stocks is that they offer relatively low dividend yields, either because they retain most of their earnings to finance expansion, because they sell at a high multiple of earnings, or both.

The companies included in the Dow Jones Industrials Average are now considered mature enterprises (of the 10 largest companies in the *Fortune 500*, seven are in the DJIA). Nevertheless, virtually all were growth stocks at one time and many continue to have superior rates of growth of sales and earnings long after they have been included in the blue chip indicator. Such issues tend to fall in the middle and bottom thirds of the Dow Jones stocks ranked by yield, and they seldom turn up high on the list of issues ranked by dividend yield.

A portfolio composed of, say, Merck, Hewlett Packard, Boeing, Disney, Altria, Wal-Mart, McDonald's, Intel, Microsoft, and Home Depot (all of which have been added to the DJIA since 1972) might well have more than held its own against trading the highest yielding issues over the past 25 years. However, there are many Lockheeds and Grummans for every Boeing; countless Tastee-Freezes for every McDonald's, etc. Few analysts, if any, can consistently identify which competitor will prevail in advance. Waiting until a company has emerged from the pack often means buying it just when it is most richly priced and its growth is on the verge of slowing down. Although many fortunes have been built on a buy-and-hold strategy of superior growth stocks, many others have been frittered away in the search for the winners.

The HYD strategy is not one of buy-and-hold—much of its efficacy comes from buying low and selling high. Following a consistent and disciplined program of investing in the highest-yielding Dow stocks means that relatively overvalued issues will be routinely weeded out of one's holdings and replaced with undervalued issues.

What If Everyone Did It?

An often expressed concern about HYD strategies in general is that they could lose their efficacy if they became widely followed by investors. The simple answer to this concern is that it is most unlikely to happen.

One might well call positions in HYD stocks "super-large-capitalization value stocks." Amazing as it may seem, the market capitalization (prices per share times the number of shares outstanding) of the 30 DJIA stocks is more than $3.5 trillion, or roughly 20 percent of the value of all 5,000 or so publicly traded stocks. It would take a very large amount of buying power following HYD strategies to make much of a difference.

More fundamentally, any HYD strategy goes against many basic aspects of human nature. These include not only such powerful emotions as fear and greed, but also the love affairs that many investors have with their holdings and the belief that becoming, or not becoming, a stockholder will have an effect on the company, the natural environment, politics, the world, etc. The fact is that, for all but the largest and most energetic stockholders, "the stock doesn't know you own it." A successful HYD investor need not even have any idea of what the companies do. Very few investors are willing to adopt such an attitude, and we doubt that HYD strategies will ever be followed by more than a tiny minority.

Even if an increased popularity of HYD strategies did make a difference, that difference presumably would be to narrow the variation between the higher- and lower-yielding issues in the DJIA, thereby diminishing, but probably not eliminating, the advantage of an HYD strategy. It always will be possible to rank the issues by yield, and, while the advantage of investing in the highest-yielding stocks might diminish somewhat, there is no reason to believe it would vanish completely.

Discipline is Essential

If you check out the highest-yielding issues in the Dow with a full-service brokerage firm, you will probably be told to avoid them—they are where they are because of some sort of tale of woe. Just remember that these are very large companies with assets in the billions (very often these assets are held in many countries around the globe). The essence of an HYD strategy is to get you to invest in issues that are unattractive to most investors and sell them when they return to favor. There is no reason or magic in an annual review and portfolio realignment at year-end, the most common approach, or at any other time of year.

Because common-stock portfolios that reflect HYD stock selection strategies will have a considerable overlap (*i.e.,* they will hold many issues in common) and because all stocks tend to move together over any given time frame, their returns will be essentially similar. Although our studies have indicated that buying the four highest-yielding Dow stocks and holding them for 18 months provided the best combination of return and risk (volatility) in the past, there is little reason to believe that it will be the very best approach in the near-term, or even the long-term, future. The fact is that variations between one strategy and another will mainly reflect chance, *provided* the strategies have the following elements in common:

1) Purchases should be limited to the highest-yielding issues in the DJIA, and

2) Once purchased, a given issue should be held until a predetermined criterion has been met.

When the parameters of a given strategy have been established, they should be strictly followed. Attempts to outguess the market on an *ad hoc* basis usually fail. For example, holding off on the purchase of a stock that meets the criteria you have set for yourself because you have a poor opinion of the company, or because it has been the subject of a rash of unfavorable news and comment in the press, often means missing an excellent buying opportunity. Similarly, one should not succumb to the temptations to sell an issue simply because it has increased in price and is no longer high on the list of dividend yielders. Very often such price moves continue much longer and farther than seemed possible at the bottom.

APPENDIX B
SELECTED MUTUAL FUNDS

THE mutual funds listed in the table on pp. 78-79 may be useful to investors in developing their own passive investment portfolios. The funds in this listing were selected because they are not subject to loads or marketing fees, and their expense ratios are well below industry averages. The funds are listed, in each category, by the average market capitalization of their holdings, shown in billions of dollars. Among open-end mutual funds we have limited ourselves to those offered by:

Vanguard Group	Dimensional Fund
P.O. Box 1110	Advisors
Valley Forge, PA	1299 Ocean Avenue
19482	Santa Monica CA 90401
800-871-3879	301-395-8000
www. vanguard.com	www.dfafunds.com

Vanguard Funds may be purchased directly from Vanguard or through some brokerage firms, usually with a commission or trading fee. Dimensional Fund Advisors does not offer shares of its funds directly to individual investors, but since 1989 they have made their funds available to investors who are clients of selected fee-only investment advisors. Dimensional believes that these independent advisors offer the expertise required to develop long-term investment solutions for individual investors and function as a buffer against short-term traders who can drive up costs for other holders of a given fund.

We have also included selected exchange-traded funds, or ETFs, which may be purchased through brokers at their usual commission rates. Unlike open-ended mutual funds, they may be traded whenever exchange is open, using limits, stop orders, etc. All data are as of December 31, 2006. The price is determined in the market, but experience indicates that arbitrageurs keep it very close to the NAV of a share.

ETFs often have lower expense ratios than open-end funds, but some observers believe that holding ETFs creates temptation to engage in short-term trading.

	Ticker	Average Market Cap ($billions)	Number of Holdings	—Ratios of Price to— Cash Flow	Book Value	Earnings	Expense Ratio	Turnover Ratio
Growth								
iShares SP 500 Growth	IVW	59,192	311	12.8	3.7	18.3	0.18	12
iShares S&P 500*	IVV	53,062	501	11.1	2.9	16.8	0.10	7
Vanguard 500 Index*	VFINX	50,558	513	10.9	2.8	16.7	0.18	7
Vanguard Growth Index	VIGRX	35,871	423	13.9	3.7	20.9	0.22	23
iShares R1000 Growth	IWF	34,261	684	13.9	4.0	20.8	0.20	18
Value								
Vanguard Value Index	VIVAX	49,881	416	8.8	2.3	14.3	0.21	21
iShares SP 500 Value	IVE	47,790	352	9.4	2.4	15.6	0.18	7
iShares R1000 Value	IWD	46,597	612	8.5	2.2	14.3	0.20	7
iShares R3000 Value	IWW	32,935	1,924	8.7	2.2	14.5	0.25	7
DFA US Large Cap. Value	DFLVX	12,776	218	7.1	1.5	14.6	0.30	9
iShares R. Midcap Value	IWS	6,996	482	7.3	2.0	15.9	0.25	11
Vanguard Mid Cap Value Index	VMVIX	6,197	261	8.8	2.0	15.1	0.25	16
iShares SP 400 Value	IJJ	3,084	285	9.7	2.0	17.0	0.25	21
Vanguard Small Cap Value Index	VISVX	1,470	978	8.5	1.8	16.1	0.23	28
iShares SP 600 Value	IJS	1,107	449	11.5	1.9	17.6	0.25	16
iShares R2000 Value	IWN	1,028	1,314	9.9	1.8	16.8	0.25	14
DFA U.S. Small Cap. Value	DFSVX	521	1,325	6.5	1.3	16.9	0.55	27
iShares Russell Microcap*	IWC	357	1,453	12.2	2.2	21.0	0.60	6
DFA U.S. Micro Cap*	DFSCX	289	2,439	9.0	1.9	18.9	0.55	37

* These funds are not constructed as value or growth—but they have the characteristics of the group in which they have been listed.

	Ticker	Average Market Cap ($billions)	Number of Holdings	—Ratios of Price to— Cash Flow	Book Value	Earnings	Expense Ratio	Turnover Ratio
Real Estate								
iShares C&S Realty	ICF	10,079	31	NA	3.6	38.8	0.35	18
iShares DJ RE Index	IYR	6,885	87	NA	3.1	32.2	0.60	19
Vanguard REIT Index	VGSIX	5,395	107	NA	2.9	35.5	0.21	17
DFA Real Estate Securities	DFREX	5,477	116	NA	2.9	35.1	0.37	3
International								
Vanguard European Stock Index	VEURX	37,478	623	9.0	3.4	14.6	0.27	6
Vanguard Intl Growth	VWIGX	29,401	144	11.4	3.5	17.2	0.55	45
Vanguard Intl Value	VTRIX	28,327	230	8.0	2.6	13.4	0.45	36
DFA Large Cap International	DFALX	26,853	1,606	7.5	2.7	15.7	0.29	4
DFA Intl Value	DFIVX	21,817	687	NA	2.1	13.7	0.44	15
DFA Intl Small Cap Value	DISVX	712	2,524	8.0	1.3	14.0	0.70	13
DFA Intl Small Company	DFISX	627	4,398	8.6	1.8	16.1	0.56	NA
Emerging Markets								
Vanguard Emerging Market Index	VEIEX	8,934	853	7.6	2.4	14.5	0.42	26
DFA Emerging Markets	DFEMX	5,838	608	0.6	0.2	1.6	0.61	10
DFA Emerging Markets Value	DFEVX	784	1,801	2.4	0.6	8.5	0.63	9
DFA Emerging Markets Small Cap	DEMSX	329	2,087	1.4	0.6	7.5	0.81	18
Gold								
iShares Comex Gold Trust	IAU	——These Exchange-Traded Funds hold gold bullion——						0.4
streetTRACKS Gold Shares	GLD							0.4

	Ticker	Net Assets $MM	Number of Holdings	Pct. Assets in Top 10 Holdings	Effective Duration[1]	Minimum Initial Purchase	Expense Ratio (%)	Turnover Ratio (%)
Bond Funds								
Vanguard Short-Term Investmt Grade[2]	VFSTX	10,377	874	7.88	1.70	3,000	0.21	31
iShares Lehman 1-3 Treasury Notes	SHY	5,662	30	58.94	1.80	-	0.15	83
Vanguard Total Bond Index	VBMFX	23,769	10,299	9.44	4.60	3,000	0.20	59
Vanguard Intermediate Bond Index	VBIIX	2,929	856	27.12	5.90	3,000	0.18	76
iShares Lehman 7-10	IEF	1,787	14	93.01	6.70	-	0.15	94

[1] Duration is an estimate of the effect of a 1 percentage point change on a fund's NAV.
[2] This fund is actively managed (it does not track an index).

Selected Correlations

Monthly Data Jan. 1988-Dec. 2006

	S&P 500	Russell 1000 Value	Russell 2000 Value	Wilshire All REIT	MSCI EAFE	MSCI Emerging Mkts.	Gold Bullion	5 Year T Notes
S&P 500	1.00							
Russell 1000 Value	0.91	1.00						
Russell 2000 Value	0.69	0.75	1.00					
Wilshire All REIT	0.34	0.46	0.65	1.00				
MSCI EAFE	0.62	0.57	0.49	0.25	1.00			
MSCI Emerging Markets	0.59	0.55	0.59	0.31	0.58	1.00		
Gold bullion (EOM)	-0.15	-0.12	-0.03	0.04	0.11	0.10	1.00	
5-Year Treasury Notes	0.06	0.08	-0.05	0.08	0.00	-0.14	-0.01	1.00

To buy publications or find out more about the American Institute for Economic Research please contact us at:

American Institute for Economic Research
250 Division Street, PO Box 1000
Great Barrington, Massachusetts 01230

Phone: (413) 528-1216
Fax: (413) 528-0103

aierpubs@aier.org
www.aier.org

Call or visit our website for pricing.